5DAYS
to a new self

by

Terry Hargrave, Ph.D., LMFT, and Sharon Hargrave, LMFT

Five Days to a New Self

Published by The Hideaway Foundation
1800 S. Washington St., Ste. 215
Amarillo, TX 79102

Details in some anecdotes and stories have been changed to protect the identities of the persons involved.

ISBN 978-0-692-60162-4

Published in the United States of America

2016—First Edition

Dedication

To our amazing children:

Matthew Alan Curtis
Halley Anne Curtis
Peter Sloan Hargrave
Katherine Elizabeth Hargrave

Their personhoods bless us and are new every day.

Contents

PREFACE

Brand-new. You know the feeling: The feeling of sitting in a new car where everything is clean and there isn't a scratch on this magnificent piece of machinery. Or maybe it is the feeling of putting on a new dress or shirt that makes you look more stylish than you did minutes before. Or maybe it is giving the latest game or program software a test run where everything about the new technology is so much easier and faster that you can't believe you did entertainment or work the old way.

Brand-new can feel really good. No wonder we desire the feeling so.

We remember a wonderful moment after the birth of our first child, Halley Anne. There we were, sitting in a dimly lit hospital room and resting peacefully after a long labor and birth. And there was our brand-new daughter resting in our arms, calm, secure, and whole. Her tiny fingers and toes, her full eyebrows, and her beautifully shaped mouth and lips—all were perfect. Our new little one, a visible testimony to our intimacy with one another, appeared unscathed by anything we had done. Seemingly, everything about her was a clean slate, both physically and emotionally.

If all of us are honest, the path we most often long for is the path to starting over and having a clean slate—turning back the clock to a previous time in our lives when we were unblemished by any physical flaws or emotional pain as a result of relationships gone wrong. But while turning back time or erasing the past is not a possibility, the feeling of being brand-new can become a reality.

We are part of a world that tries to assure us at every point, "I am okay and you are okay." In other words, we are acceptable and fine just the way we are. Furthermore, we are bombarded with the message that whatever we feel at any particular time is the deepest and most real part of ourselves. And so we are taught that we have no need to learn or change.

This book, in contrast, is about becoming new by changing the old.

Parts of you represent a giftedness and specialness that make you unique and essential to the work God wants you to accomplish in the world. But just because these parts are great does not mean you do not need to change. The Bible makes this absolutely clear. We also have parts representing the old self that are worn out and ugly and that prompt us to engage in behaviors that we regret and that usually harm others. Both our gifts and our failings exist, and both affect the way we feel and the ways we act and behave.

Becoming brand-new does not mean that we erase the past or get a total do-over. It means, rather, that we cooperate with the Holy Spirit and do the hard and painstaking work of changing our old-self habits into a new-self reality. As the apostle Paul wrote in a key passage for this book: "Put off your old self, which belongs to your former manner of life and is corrupt through deceitful desires, and…be renewed in the spirit of your minds, and…put on the new self, created after the likeness of God in true righteousness and holiness" (Ephesians 4:20-24). We must learn what it is like to take off what is old and put on what is new.

If this sounds like a restoration project, then you are getting an idea of the process that is required. But here is something we can promise: when you get to the heart of what is old and wrong about the way you think about yourself and the world, and then adopt a new and peaceful way of life instead, it will feel like settling into the seat of a great new car, slipping on fashionable new clothes, or booting up amazing new software. It is possible to feel new even as your self is in the midst of restoration. We're going to show you how.

You will notice that this book is only five chapters long. Although each chapter is outlined in such a way that you can read it in a day, you should take as much time as you need to process the material and make it real to you. Is it possible to set yourself on the road to new identity in a mere five days? Absolutely! But it is not a race. Based on your style and what is most helpful to you, choose how much time you want to take in reading and processing the material.

As you are making your way through the book, be sure to work through the exercises in each chapter in order to get the full benefit of the material. Obviously, stopping to do the exercises will take more time than if you just read the chapters. Working through the exercises, however, is worth it. The effort you put out will bring the reality of the concepts home to you and will start you on your way to experiencing a new self.

We recommend that, if possible, you work through the book with a study group. If you do so, the group should be no larger than seven people, including the leader. Because the material will ask you to share stories of your life, if the groups are too big, it will become too difficult to hear from everyone. You will also want your group to meet together before you start on Day 1 so that you can get to know each other and begin to connect before diving right into the material. Have your group members set aside six weeks to meet for an hour and a half each week.

Consider the following tips:

1. Each time you open the book, say a simple prayer to God asking Him to enlighten your reading and bless your work in the exercises.

2. Read no more than one chapter per day.

3. Don't read a chapter and then go back to do the exercises afterward. Instead, work through all the exercises in each chapter *as you are reading*.

4. Take advantage of the "For Reflection" section you find at the end of each chapter. This section is designed for you to work through with a friend or your study group.

5. Practice what you have learned every day while reading.

If you follow these instructions, you will find hope and realize that change is possible. Remember, you can do the work of becoming new again! We are for you and your personhood, and there are many others, including God, who have your back in this process. We'll be explaining more about this—and much else—in the pages ahead.

Although we authored this book, it represents material that comes from a collaboration of therapists, students, friends, and fellow followers of Jesus who believe in the mission of the restoration of the self. Special thanks go to Steve and Rajan Trafton, who make many visions, including this one, come to fruition.

May God bless your work as you start Day 1.

For Reflection

1. What are your goals in studying this material?

2. What difficult things have you learned about relationships in the family or context you grew up in?

3. What are some of the best things you learned about relationships in the family or context you grew up in?

DAY ONE

--- ◆ ---

Reckoning Rightly

"Do you want to be healed?"

This is the famous question that Jesus asked the invalid by the pool of Bethesda. The man had lain by the pool for thirty-eight years, waiting and watching, hoping he could get in the pool first when the waters stirred. He believed that a miracle would happen if he could achieve the task. And Jesus asked him, "Do you want to be healed?" (John 5:6).

What a crazy question! Of course he wanted to be healed! But as we follow the story, we find that the man did not reply, "Boy, do I!" Instead, he explained to Jesus why he couldn't be the first in the waters and why it was impossible for him to access the miracle. The chance of the miracle was right before him, yet he did not recognize the opportunity of a lifetime. Even after Jesus healed him and he walked away, he showed little evidence that he was thankful for the healing. He seemed more interested in making sure that he answered the questions of the religious leaders.

We all come to the first day of working on a new self with similar preconceptions and issues. God is asking us, "Do you want to be healed?" Do we want to be healed from the nagging doubt about ourselves and the crazy behaviors we hardly understand but know are damaging to ourselves and others? Like the invalid at Bethesda, when we are given the opportunity to think and do something different, we will likely assume we are the exception or excuse our behaviors as justifiable.

The invalid was not being difficult or even especially self-focused. He was just so used to thinking about himself as an invalid and dealing with the reality of his limitations he had trouble seeing the new possibilities.

In this chapter, we will help you understand and organize the way you feel and the way you react. Try to relax and focus on the possibilities of understanding your identity and behaviors in a new way. Be open to a first step in healing into a new self. You can do this work!

Different and All the Same

We are all unique in our expressions, gifts, talents, likes, and dislikes. No two of us are the same. All of us are special in our expression of personhood and the relationships we keep.

We do, however, have a heritage that marks us as similar. For example, all of us have DNA and twenty-three pairs of chromosomes. We have a common anatomy and physiology. We also have similar brains.

Although our brains have primitive functions that keep up basic functions such as breathing and heart pumping, we have a higher-functioning part of our brain that sets the stage for us to *understand* the world. One of the basic ways we understand the world is by understanding ourselves. In other words, one of the essentials about understanding our place in the world is to understand our *identity*—how we are important and whether or not we matter.

We learn our sense of identity from the way people love us. Love is essential to the human condition from the start of life.

If caregivers do not fulfill some basic attachment needs of infants, the children will fail to develop in a normal way and, in worst-case scenarios, fail to thrive to the point where they are in danger of dying. But these care needs of the infant go way past nourishment and protection. The newborn needs a basic level of bonding that gives the assurance that he or she is important. Touching, cuddling, and a comforting voice turn on the brain of the infant, assuring him or her of the love that can only come from attachment. In simple terms, we learn about who we are through the way we are loved in basic relationships.

We like to think of love in terms of three types identified most often in the ancient Greek language: *eros, phileo,* and *agape.*

We most often think of *eros* love as an erotic or romantic love, but it is actually a love fascinated or consumed with thoughts about the beloved. For instance, think of the first time you were in love. Chances are, you could not get the thought of that person out of your head. You likely wrote his or her name in combination with your name over and over. You might remember holding hands with this person for the first time. Maybe you didn't want to wash your hand in order to not lose the scent of your beloved. When in *eros* love, we are fascinated with our beloved to the point that we must have this person and only this person, because no one else will do. The beloved is like the water to our thirst, and nothing else can quench our need.

Parents love their children in this way. Parents are fascinated with every aspect of who their children are and what they are becoming. Parents consider themselves lucky to be parenting their children and find that no other child can replace *their* child.

How does this feel to a child who receives this kind of *eros* love? He or she feels unique and irreplaceable. No one or nothing can take his or her place in the eyes of the ones who love. This reality makes a deep impact on the child's identity and it immediately teaches the child that he or she is special. No one else is like this child, who is irreplaceable to those who love him or her.

God extends this type of love to us, communicating that we are special. Paul quotes Hosea to this effect:

> Those who were not my people I will call "my people,"
> and her who was not beloved I will call "beloved."
> (*Romans 9:25;* see *Hosea 2:23*)

We fascinate God. He *wants* us. We are irreplaceable to Him, and therefore our identity should claim and acknowledge our specialness.

But love's effect on our identity does not stop there. Our identity is also greatly influenced by *phileo* love. This normally has been identified as a brotherly love, but it can more easily be understood as a friendship love.

Think about your best friend in the world. Among the many things the friend gives you, such as loyalty, faithfulness, fun, and spontaneity, there should be a sense that you could always count on this friend. In many cases where you don't live close to your best friend, you may go days, weeks, and even months without talking to him or her. Yet, if you were at the end of your rope, you would feel that you could call him or her and this friend would be there for you.

Best friends—friends who love us with this type of companionate *phileo*— know us well and are there for us. In a sense, when you have experienced this type of friendship, you can never truly be alone again. You carry your friend, and your friend carries you, in a love that crosses miles of distance and years of time. This is what *phileo* love does for us. It teaches us that we truly *belong* and can never quite be alone.

Parents can certainly give this type of love to their children, but it is love that grows and is usually based on true companionship and friendship. We remember how surprising it was when we discovered that our son and daughter had skills and talents that we ourselves do not possess. As they grew, however, it was also clear that they were developing outlooks and opinions on life that we did not have. Our children's identities forced us to realize they were not clones of us but rather were separate and unique individuals. They were people we had to get to know, appreciate, and love the same way we had to get to know friends.

Our children bring things to the table we do not have, and when we embrace them with *phileo*, we appreciate them and enjoy them for the friendship they bring into our lives. Parents really communicate *belonging* to children when they befriend them in a mutual companionship.

Ruth had this type of companionate commitment toward Naomi. Ruth said to the older woman, "Do not urge me to leave you or to return from following you. For where you go I will go, and where you lodge I will lodge. Your people shall be my people, and your God my God. Where you die I will die, and there will I be buried" (*Ruth 1:16-17*). In this beautiful expression when both women were left destitute without family or hope, Ruth made the proclamation of what it takes to be a good friend—following, staying with, sharing values and beliefs, and being committed to the end.

God loves us in this manner. As both Old and New Testaments say, "He will not leave you or forsake you" (*Deuteronomy 31:6; see Hebrews 13:5*).

Eros teaches us that we are special and unique, and *phileo* teaches us that we belong. These are essential aspects of healthy identity, but the third type of love holds the power to convince us just how much we are worth.

Agape has often been taught in our culture as a love of acceptance no matter what we do. *Agape* love does have this commitment of loyalty and acceptance, but that is not the primary factor. Sacrifice is the most important element in *agape*.

We often see this sacrificial love played out with parents when they sacrifice their needs for their children's wants. You see, sacrificial love comes not out of our abundance but out of our exclusive interest to see the beloved survive and thrive *at our expense*.

Imagine yourself and a dear friend in a concentration camp where both of you are on the edge of death. You have food for only one. If you eat the food, you survive. Or if your friend eats the food, he or she survives. If you split the food, both of you will die. *Agape* love says to the other, "You eat the food." It is a love that costs the lover something dear, perhaps even life itself.

Parents often try to give us this type of love and often succeed. But many times, parents make sacrifices of their time, money, and freedom, only to keep an account of those sacrifices and hold it over their children's heads. How many times have you heard a version of the following from your own parent or some

15

close friend's parent: "Look at all the sacrifices I made for you. You owe me!" The reality is, when parents give in this manner, expecting that their children will perform better or pay them back in some way, it is not sacrificial giving at all. It is, at best, conditional giving.

There is a problem with conditional giving, as it puts the recipient in a position of obligation or perpetual performance. If I owe someone for what he or she gave me, then I am always on the hook to please this person or to perform to his or her expectations. My worth, therefore, is always dependent upon how I perform to the giver's expectations or pay the giver back what I was given. Guilt and failure are regular feelings that accompany this kind of conditional giving.

Not so with true *agape*, or sacrificial, giving. In this type of love, the giver recognizes the extraordinary worth in the recipient. The giver is not looking to be paid back but instead is looking for the recipient to recognize that the amount of sacrifice is in accord with the value of the recipient.

We have no better example for this type of sacrificial giving than God's sacrifice of Jesus. In the words of the most familiar passage in the Bible, "God so loved the world, that he gave his only Son, that whoever believes in him should not perish but have eternal life. For God did not send his Son into the world to condemn the world, but in order that the world might be saved through him" (*John 3:16-17*). How does God benefit from this type of love? It is hard to say that there is a direct benefit to God. The primary benefit comes to us who believe, and the amount of sacrifice made tells us that we are indeed worth much to God. We are—as hard as it is to believe—at least as valuable to God as God's only Son. This is how much He values us.

What we would say, then, is that if you feel unique and special, like you belong and are not alone and feel valuable and worthy, then you have been richly loved and you have a healthy self-identity. But even in those of us who grew up with great families and super parents or caregivers, we likely didn't come through with our sense of identity unscathed. This is due to several reasons.

First, none of our parents were perfect. Even in those areas where we can identify our parents as having solid *eros, phileo,* and *agape,* they did not always come through in communicating and caring for us in just the way needed. All of us have imperfect identities because the people who were in charge of loving us were imperfect themselves in spite of their good intentions.

Second, and sometimes more importantly, our parents were not the only ones who spoke into our identities. Coaches, teachers, or important friends sometimes make people feel common or average, on the outside, or as if their worth is dependent upon their performance.

For instance, one woman we spoke with had no complaints about the love she received within the household she grew up in, but she clearly identified the fact that she had trouble believing in herself because of a gymnastics class when she was a child. She said, "When I was seven, there was nothing I was more excited about than gymnastics. I wore my outfit everywhere and I dreamed that I was going to be an Olympian. One day, during a parent watch session, I overheard the teacher speaking with parents across the gym while we were warming up on the other side. The teacher said, 'All these girls have talent!' and I was so proud that I went right into a cartwheel. Then I heard her say, 'Well, maybe not all,' and several parents laughed. I never could trust myself since then that, when I thought I was good at something, I was actually good. I never felt I was good enough to belong."

It was just a short gymnastics class, and yet the impact on this woman's identity was enormously powerful. For us, too, it may be small shortcomings or little incidents that injured our identities along the way. It is wise for us to recognize where these pains, doubts, and injuries originated so we can better understand ourselves. Later on in the chapter we will also learn about other life situations that can also cause us to struggle with issues pertaining to our own safety and issues of trust.

Some people, however, grew up in places where violations of love were quite large. It can be confusing at times because many parents or caregivers can do quite remarkable things, such as providing a great place to live and wonderful opportunities for their children. If physical or emotional abuse is present, however, it can leave children feeling unwanted and like they do not belong. Often this kind of abuse is passed from generation to generation and is damaging to the sense of identity for many. If someone has grown up feeling unloved and alone, this will be the most dominant and powerful message he or she will feel.

Our brain mostly organizes around the negative or threatening in order to try to ward off possible threat. The pain of the abuse can be such that it wiped away the positive messages a family can give in other ways.

For you, wherever the message came from in terms of your identity—from caregivers, parents, peers, mentors, or life situations—the message has likely remained written on your brain. Whenever this message of your faulty identity gets confirmed from past thoughts, present situations, or circumstances, you likely will feel the primary message about your identity come crashing back into your brain. It is helpful to not only identify these messages about your identity but also to understand and track down where some of those messages originated. The first exercise will help you with this identification.

EXERCISE 1

Identifying your primary emotions about your identity

1. When you are emotionally upset or unsettled, how do you usually feel about yourself? (An alternative question may be "What are the messages you received about your identity from family or friends?") Circle one or two emotions that best describe how you feel.

Unloved	Worthless	Rejected	Unappreciated
Unworthy	Devalued	Unaccepted	Hopeless
Insignificant	Defective	Unwanted	
Alone	Inadequate	Abandoned	

2. In thinking about how you feel about your identity when emotionally upset (or what you were taught about your identity from family or friends), is there a better word or two that describes the feeling? Write these words down.

_____

3. Think about either the *first time* you remember having these feelings about your identity or the *most recent* time you had these feelings. Make a note of these feelings and the effect the feelings and incident had on your identity or sense of self.

_____

The Other Pillar of Attachment

The Beatles famously sang, "All you need is love." Fifty years later, we know that, while love is great, it is insufficient for human beings to be rightly attached. Trust and safety in relationships are also absolutely essential if one is to be healthy.

Identity is not the only factor at work in the human brain. The brain is also trying to make sense of how to go about this interactive game called relationships.

Relationships, you see, require at least two people who are engaged in mutual giving to one another and taking from one another. For example, in relationships with friends, there are things we rightly are expected to give to them because we are friends. We give them a listening ear when they want to be heard, care when they are hurt, or congratulation when they are overjoyed. We laugh with them and cry with them, and many times we give them time because we care about and enjoy our friends.

Although these behaviors are voluntary, the truth is that our friends have come to expect these behaviors from us. And we expect our friends to behave in the same way toward us. In other words, as we engage with our friends, giving care, compassion, time, and presence, we think it is fair to expect them to act the same way. In fact, because we give to our friends, we actually feel entitled to take the care, compassion, time, and presence that they give to us.

All relationships have this element of give-and-take. This balance, over a long period of time, builds a sense of trustworthiness or safety in the relational partners. For instance, let us look at a place of employment. As you can see in the chart below, from the employee's perspective, it is fair that he or she brings competent skills to the job, puts in substantial effort and work, performs tasks well and achieves goals, behaves toward others in a kind and respectful way, and is consistent or predictable in these behaviors. If the employee behaves this way, then he or she has every right to expect that the employer will provide an atmosphere of respect and provide fair compensation for the work performed. Note that what is given by both parties does not have to be the same thing, but it has to be judged as fair or balanced.

Given By Employee to Employer	Given by Employer to Employee:
1. Skills and talents	1. Respect
2. Substantial effort	2. Fair compensation for work
3. Performs well/achieves goals	
4. Kind and respectful to others	
5. Predictable/consistent	

If this employee-employer relationship goes on for a substantial period of time, the fair balance of give-and-take produces a wonderful resource of trust or safety in the relationship. The employer likely feels the employee is consistent and will do his or her best without threats or heavy supervision. Because the employee has been compensated fairly by the employer, he or she knows what to expect from the work situation and feels comfortable doing his or her work. In this balanced or trustworthy relationship, both the employee and employer are not worried about being taken advantage of or being harmed by the other, and both are free to concentrate on their own part of the giving.

The reality is that we are born knowing things should be balanced and safe. This innate understanding is like an internal gyroscope that informs us when things are out of balance and we are being unfairly treated or are treating others unfairly. For instance, how long do you think the employee would work for the employer if he or she were not treated with respect or stopped being compensated? How long would the employer put up with the employee if he or she simply stopped showing up for work? Whenever an imbalance in the give-and-take developed, both parties would immediately sense it was unfair and both would likely move to start protecting themselves from the other. The relationship simply would not be safe anymore and both would stop giving.

This is why safety and trustworthiness are such important factors to the human brain. To give to another, we have to have reasonable hope that the relationship will be safe and balanced. If not, we will be cast out on our own, fearful to be in relationship because we will be taken advantage of, and terrified because we might not know how to meet our own needs without another.

We were built for safe relationships, and life becomes difficult if we have no one for whom we mutually care. Wise Solomon put it this way: "Two are better than one, because they have a good reward for their toil. For if they fall, one will lift up his fellow. But woe to him who is alone when he falls and has not another to lift him up! Again, if two lie together, they keep warm, but how can one keep warm alone? And though a man might prevail against one who is alone, two will withstand him—a threefold cord is not quickly broken" (*Ecclesiastes 4:9-12*).

We require safety to survive and thrive, and there is no way to feel safe apart from the context of relationship. When those relationships are balanced, we are able to stretch our comfort zone with others because we have the ability to trust that others will give to us. In turn, trustworthiness allows us to give to others with an unfettered feeling and no fear.

But hold on a moment! It might be all well and good to see how this safety and trustworthiness stuff works with friends and employers, but how about parents and children? When we were first born into a family, we did not have much ability to give to our parents. How did we achieve balance, safety, and trustworthiness in those relationships?

At first glance, family relationships between parents and children (successive generations) look out of whack because we expect that children—at least when they are young—cannot give the same level of care given to them. As the illustration below demonstrates, a young child requires much from a parent and owes the parent nothing.

Given to the Child From the Parent:	Given to the Parent from the Child:
1. Love	1. Nothing
2. Nurture	
3. Time	
4. Respect	
5. Predictability	

You might look at the illustration and think, *It looks like a good deal for the child but not so good for the parent!* You would, however, likely say that the relationship is fair because the young child is not yet capable of giving to the parent. Perhaps you would think that the young child, as he or she grows, will owe the parent love and nurture later in life. Some people reason this way, but they are missing an essential element in the intergenerational family. It is not fair and balanced because of what the child will eventually give back to the parent but rather because of what the child will eventually give to his or her own children.

To understand this, think in terms of the parent once being a child. He or she was presumably given love, nurture, and care. The parent, when he or she was a child, did not have to give back the love and care to his or her parent but simply drank in the benefit. As this child grew into a parent, however, he or she then was required to give the same kinds of resources previously given by his or her own parents. And so it goes, generation by generation.

Unlike a friendship or marriage, in a parent-child relationship balance and safety are not achieved by giving directly back to the person who gave to you. Rather, in intergenerational families, the balance is maintained by giving the resources to the youngest generation, and when it is the right time, those individuals will pass along the resources to the next generation of children. It is still balanced and safe, but it is balanced in the family by paying it forward.

When families work in this balanced and safe fashion, it is a beautiful thing. The intergenerational group may even become stronger, more predictable, and more stable with each new generation. In these situations, it is indeed trustworthy and safe.

But of course, not all families work in this manner. In some families, the opposite happens.

That was the case with a twenty-eight-year-old man who recounted his growing-up years in his family. He said, "As long as I could remember, it was my responsibility to take care of my mother. My father left us before I was born, and my mother was so fragile that she was overwhelmed by everything. One of my first memories as a toddler was comforting my mother on our front step when she was saying she was planning to kill herself. By age six, I was the one responsible for caring for my brother. By age eight, I was stealing money at school so we could eat. By age ten, I was working at any job I could find to keep my mother and brother functioning. I do not remember one person in my life connected with my family ever taking care of me just for my good."

In this man's case, he did not receive love, nurture, and care as a young child but was instead required to give it to the very person who should have provided for him. Certainly this was an untrustworthy situation for him, and this lack of safety affected him in future relationships. Because he had already given love, care, and nurture to his family and had no trustworthy resource for himself, he became isolated as an adult and felt as if any relationship—friendship, romantic connection, or family—was a threat and a drag on him. He felt alone, fearful, and empty and would cover these feelings by drinking too much almost on a nightly basis. He was not a bad guy, and people wanted to be his friend. His early unsafe and untrustworthy family experiences, however, set the stage for him to have no resources to give to future relationships. Every relationship felt unsafe to him because his first relationships in his family were unsafe and little could change because he trusted no one.

It is not just the feelings of balance and safety that we carry with us in the current relationships we experience; we also have an intricate memory of our first and most important relationships and the trustworthiness those interactions provided, or the destructive impact they had on us. In just the same way, our brains are deeply impacted by the way we were loved and our resulting identity, we also have long lasting feelings that are cued when it comes to safety and trustworthiness of relationships. And these feelings regarding love and safety tend to stay with us lifelong because they were put there in the most important and often the first relationships we experienced.

To understand better the impact on our feelings around the area of safety, work through the next exercise on page 25.

EXERCISE 2
Identifying your primary emotions about your safety

1. When you are emotionally upset or unsettled, how do you usually feel about the situation or relationship? (An alternative question may be "What are the words that best describe the messages about relationships you received from family or friends?") Circle one or two emotions best describing how you feel.

Unsafe	Fearful	Disconnected	Unknown
Unfair	Powerless	Betrayed	Unsure
Used	Out of control	Insecure	
Guilty	Vulnerable	Unable to measure up	

2. In thinking about how you feel about relationships when emotionally upset or the messages you received from family or friends that describe your relationships, is there a better word or two that describes the feeling? Write these words down.

_____

3. Think about either the *first time* you remember having these feelings about your relationships or the *most recent* time you had these feelings in relationships. Make a note of the feelings and situation and the effect it had on your beliefs or sense of safety.

Most often, feelings of lack of safety come from our families where we grew up or other very important relationships, such as those with teachers or mentors. But sometimes they come from traumatic events or disasters.

A good example of this is rooted in my (Sharon's) history. I was the fourth of four children and the only girl. I was born in southern California, where my father was an advertising executive and my mother stayed at home to raise us. It was, in many ways, an idyllic way to grow up, with my family having fun and caring for one another in a beautiful place. I still have home movies of my brothers and dad playing baseball or tennis, going to Disneyland, and sharing life with popular Hollywood types. I am sure our family life at the time was not perfect, but I know that I felt safe and passionately loved, just like a princess.

That was until the wheels started coming off in my family.

Unknown to us, my father was bipolar, meaning that he periodically went through mood swings between high energy and depression. He spent almost all of his life on the high-energy side of those swings and had only two significant depressive periods. But during the second depressive episode, when he was having work trouble, he made the devastating decision to commit suicide. I was three at the time of his death. My mother was left with four children to raise and made the courageous decision to move to Texas, where she had an older brother. Somehow she started stringing together a normal life for us in a new place, but much of the fun was gone with our loss and displacement.

A little over a year later, my oldest brother, Bruce, came home from school reporting that he was not feeling well. Thinking it was the flu, my mother kept him home from school the next day and put him to bed. The next day, in the evening, Bruce said that he thought maybe something more serious was wrong with him. My mother called the doctor immediately and made arrangements to take Bruce in for tests the next morning. Unfortunately, Bruce died in the night from acute leukemia. In 1961, with such short notice, it is doubtful that my brother could have been saved even if he had been hospitalized when he first started complaining about symptoms. But the fact was that he was gone.

Within fourteen months, my once loving and trustworthy family had been reduced by two members in harsh and tragic ways.

Somehow we were able to survive. Mostly, it is a testimony to my mother that she was able to resource us kids with love and safety amid tragedy to keep us moving in a good direction. And many things about my family were still positive and solid throughout my grade-school years. I remember great family vacations, trips to watch my brothers play tennis, and laughter around the dinner table. We were still a family that knew how to love one another and depend on one another. But we also knew that life could deal you blows that could erase any sense of pre-dictability and control in an instance. Life felt unsafe, not because my family was irresponsible, but just because life could be tragic.

And we were not yet done with family tragedy.

Ten years after my father's suicide, my next oldest brother, David, was a senior at the University of Oklahoma. David was a fun-loving guy who was popular with many. We received a call on Mother's Day that David and his date had not returned from a Saturday night outing. This was not like either one of them, and so my mother, my brother, and I drove to Norman, Oklahoma. When we arrived, we were notified that David and his date had been found, murdered. Their bodies had been left in the trunk of a car outside of town.

If life had not already proved that there was no control and that tragedy can happen at any moment, this murder proved to us that we were indeed in an un-safe world. There were few limits to the bad things that could happen to a good family. I was deeply loved in my family, and I could depend on them…that is, if they did not get depressed, commit suicide, contract a terminal illness, or have a maniac take their lives. The trauma and tragedy of life proved that I was unsafe, and it held a real possibility that I would be left alone. These two realities under-standably left me feeling fearful.

Your feelings are just as understandable. Whether your identity and sense of safety were damaged in the family you grew up in, by important people such as peers, mentors, coaches, or teachers, or by the tragedy of life, you have a story that has shaped your early experiences or life. You hold on to these feelings, not because they are pleasing and helpful, but because they have become part of the programming in your brain.

When something happens to us where we are upset or emotionally disregu-lated, it is like our brains go back to the basic program and these feelings about our identity and sense of safety are retriggered.[1] We call these important feelings about identity and sense of safety primary emotions. You can think of them as "hot buttons," "automatic feelings," or "amygdala hijacks," but the fact is that these primary emotions happen again and again whenever you get upset or emotionally disregulated in interactions or everyday life.

EXERCISE 3
**Compiling a List of Your Primary Emotions About
Your Identity and Safety**

1. Take a few moments and think about your own story. This story may be of how you grew up, where you went to school, or how your life and relationships have developed recently. Review the story in your mind and think about how this narrative has shaped your identity and sense of safety in relationships.

2. Now review the words that you circled and/or wrote down in the previous two exercises, pages 19 and 25. In light of the story you just reviewed, do these words describe your feelings? Are there any words not in the list you can think of that are more descriptive of your emotions. If so, write these words down as well.

3. Take a few moments and list the words from both exercises in the box below. Try to only include the most important words that pertain to your feelings about your identity or sense of safety, limiting yourself to a maximum of five words.

Feelings
1. _____
2. _____
3. _____
4. _____
5. _____

If We Could Just Stop Ourselves

Tracking down our primary emotions helps us understand our basic programming. But understanding is not enough to produce change in our behaviors. The reality is, we are programmed to receive love and trustworthiness, and when we do not receive them in a consistent manner, we react. We know this reaction best as a "fight or flight" reaction.

In the brain, we have an area called the *midbrain* or the *limbic system*. This is a less-developed part of our brain that takes care of more automatic functions, such as basic processing, basic emotions, and physiological stabilization. It is, to a large extent, a non-thinking part of our brain. It interprets information on a basic level to make sure we are prepared to react if we are threatened or under stress. If you saw a grizzly bear attacking, this part of your brain would rightly read the situation as extremely dangerous and threatening. Within a split second, your brain would mobilize you to react by either mounting some kind of *fight* against the bear or to commence a *flight* from the animal.

Such a response is easy to see when a threat is clear, such as when a grizzly bear is attacking, but it is much more subtle when the threat or stress is a challenge to our basic sense of identity or safety. It is important to remember, however, that the midbrain is not good at reading subtlety; this part of the brain reads things more in black and white, as either threatening or nonthreatening. When your identity or safety is challenged, your midbrain interprets the stress as a threat and mobilizes you for a fight or flight reaction.

Listen to what people say with regard to the threat and their reactions in relationships:

- "I felt like I was all alone in the world and no one cared about me in the least. I just crawled into my shell and kept to myself."

- "My supervisor was so angry and accusatory, saying things that were not true about me. I just couldn't take it anymore, so I stood up, slammed my fist down on the desk, and started yelling back."

- "You can't trust people. They may not mean to, but they will always let you down. I just make sure that I only depend on myself and never make myself vulnerable by depending on someone else."

- "I get overwhelmed sometimes to the point where I don't want to face any more issues. At best, I go to bed and pull the blanket over my head. At worst, I go on a binge and drink for days."

In all of the situations above, you can see where the people had a challenge to their sense of identity or safety and then moved to some kind of fight or flight reaction. The point is, however, that *they all moved to react.* This is the way the brain is programmed, and it is a way we all cope with threats in our relationships and world.

Being reactive, however, can get in the way of having good and healthy relationships. It can even create more damage. And so, before acting, we have to learn to reckon rightly with what's going on.

Rightly Reckoning, Part One

I (Terry) grew up in a family that had some destructive patterns of interactions that had been passed from generation to generation. I interpreted that reality in such a way that I felt unloved, unwanted, and unable to measure up to expectations. As a result, my fight-or-flight reactivity took over in an effort to cope with the stress.

First, I had a flight reaction and pulled back into myself. I assumed there was something deeply wrong with me and there was little hope that anyone would love me, because I was so hopeless as a human being. I withdrew into myself, was negative about the prospect of relationships, and was extraordinarily anxious about people discovering how inadequate I really was.

This, of course, got me nowhere in life. So even though I had this initial reaction of withdrawing into myself, I began to try to compensate for my inadequacies by performing. I worked hard in doing sports, being funny, and eventually achieving academically. I still felt hopeless and inadequate as a person, but I thought that maybe I could fool or hide from others by looking competent on the athletic field or in the classroom.

Maybe this describes you also. Trying to compensate by performing well is a common trait. But as performers know, you are only as good as your last performance.

I often do workshops where evaluation forms are passed out. I am a good teacher, and so it is not unusual for 95 percent of my evaluations to be overwhelmingly positive. I will often receive comments like "Best workshop I have ever attended" or "This material is life changing." Yet these ratings or comments do not get my attention. I skip over them. I most often will spend my time focused on the 5 percent of the evaluations that are not positive or the comments that are critical of some aspect of the teaching. And after I have put in all the effort to perform the workshop well and get the positive feedback, how do I react to this small amount of negative information? Two directions: I either will slink back into my comfortable position of feeling like a hopeless human being who is a failure or I will become aggressively angry about the people who did not respond positively.

It is understandable why I react the way I do. After all, I feel deeply unloved, unwanted, and unable to measure up. It makes sense that I would beat myself up with shame, saying I am no good. It makes sense that I would try to perform myself into a better identity by impressing people. It makes sense, after I work so hard to perform and yet fail, that I would either get depressed or angry. It is *totally understandable*. But the hard reality is that, when I shame myself or try to control others' perceptions through performing or getting angry, I am doing damage to my own sense of self and my ability to do relationships well.

In our work with families and individuals over the years, we see four main categories of reactivity or coping with primary emotions. These categories are *blame, shame, control,* and *escape*. It is important to note that blame and control are aggressive, or fight, reactions, while shame and escape are flight reactions. As you see in the illustration below, we have primary emotions that result in reactivity.

Violations of Love (Identity) and Trustworthiness (Safety)

Results In...

Primary Emotions of Feeling Unloved and/or Unsafe

Leads to Reactivity of...

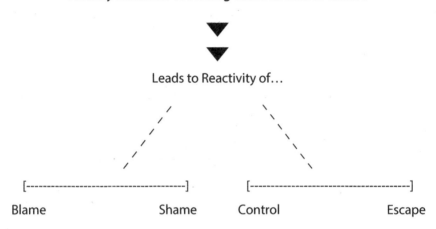

Blame   Shame   Control   Escape

Let's look closer at these four categories of reaction.

Blame.

Blame is a reaction for the pain felt, and it is common for those who find themselves reacting this way to feel deeply entitled to feel loved and safe by others. In turn, they often react in an aggressive fashion that accuses another of not providing the love and trustworthiness needed. They direct their behaviors at blaming others, being angry, raging, being sarcastic, acting arrogant, being aggressive, threatening, being retaliatory, and punishing.

The person who blames does not *feel* angry as much as he or she reacts with anger. In other words, the blamer feels unsafe or unloved (primary emotion). In reaction to these feelings, he or she tends to make demands or demean others because these others are not able to supply the identity or safety the person lacks.

The problem with blaming is that it guarantees that nothing in relationship will get better. The most aggressive forms of blame, such as threats, rage, and violence, damage others. How ironic it is that a person reacts with blame and anger because he or she feels unloved and unsafe yet in the process of the reactivity makes others feel unloved and unsafe. Worse still, the blamer knows he or she is causing damage to others, and this in turn further damages his or her own sense of identity or safety.

Shame.

A blamer will look at the fact that he or she feels unloved and/or unsafe and come to the conclusion that others are responsible for cheating him or her of the love and trustworthiness deserved. People who react with shame feel the same sense of being unloved or unsafe but come to the conclusion they *deserve* to be treated in an unloving or untrustworthy way because they are some how "bad" or "less than." In other words, a shamer believes that there is nothing unique, special, or worthy about him or her and feels that he or she does not deserve to belong or have a safe, predictable, and fair relationship. As a result, the person who reacts with shame engages in self-loathing and self-hatred.

Shame is not so much how the person feels. It is how he or she *reacts* to the primary feelings of unloved and/or unsafe.

A person who reacts with shame not only shames himself or herself; he or she often acts depressed, negative, hopeless, and inconsolable. The more you try to make a shamer feel loved and safe, the more you realize that he or she has a hole that simply cannot be filled. Often, the person who shames himself or herself will whine about how he or she is not loved and will become manipulative, sulky, or even self-harming.

It is important to remember that those who shame themselves are not simply feeling sorry for themselves any more than a blamer is an evil or vindictive person. People who react with shame feel deep pain and simply are reacting in a method of flight to blame themselves and put themselves down. They are simply human beings who are carried away with pain and reactivity.

33

Control.

We all want to believe we are competent and capable. The problem is, of course, almost none of us are actually all that capable on our own.

First, there is the reality that only God is truly in control. Listen to how God describes how he stands alone in ability:

> I am God, and there is none like me,
> declaring the end from the beginning
> and from ancient times things not yet done,
> saying, "My counsel shall stand,
> and I will accomplish all my purpose,"
> calling a bird of prey from the east,
> the man of my counsel from a far country.
> I have spoken, and I will bring it to pass;
> I have purposed, and I will do it. (*Isaiah 46:9-11*)

None of us has competency remotely rivaling God's.

Second, we are built for relationships and, as such, do not necessarily make wise decisions on our own. "Without counsel plans fail," Solomon said, "but with many advisers they succeed" (*Proverbs 15:22*). While it is not wrong to do our best, there is something insidious about trying to always be in control. It goes against who we are as relational beings.

Control (as we are discussing it) means an individual feels the same questions of identity and safety that we have discussed before. In reacting with control, however, he or she has decided to exit the normal mode of relationships and balanced give-and-take to try and make himself or herself invulnerable. In other words, the controller says, "I can only depend on myself and I can only know who I am when I do everything my way. To do less, is to put myself at risk and to give up my identity."

As a result, controllers are often performance driven and perfectionistic.

They do not take input from others well and often react in defensiveness. When they are in relationships, they often demand that everything be done their way and come across as demanding, judging, and critical. They may nag or lecture. In short, a person who is reactive by controlling seldom believes he or she is wrong and has difficulty letting other people make decisions or offer free contribution to the relationship.

I (Sharon) think of myself as a world-class controller. Given my background, this makes sense. I know the painful reality that loved ones can be snatched away from us in an instant and that we live in a world that is anything but safe. So I learned early how to react by not depending on others to take care of details and provide care for me. I reacted by making sure I knew as much as possible that everything would work out in a predictable and pleasing way. When it came to doing homework or preparing for tests in school, I would always put in the time necessary and make sure I had read every page and studied every note. Later, when I married, I always had an idea of how we needed to spend our time.

It was not that I believed I had all the answers; it was the fact that I had an overwhelming fear that things would get out of control and be unsafe and I would be left alone. So I reacted by thinking, *If I can get all my ducks in a row, and make sure everyone in my family gets their ducks in a row, I will be safe and prevent awful things happening.* But of course, not everyone in my family thought that my way was always the best way, and my agenda was not always what they wanted to do. When they would protest or act less than enthusiastic, I would blame and get angry.

Escape.

When someone is engaged in controlling behavior, it is as if the person is thinking, *What do I have to do to make sure I am safe and know who I am?* In turn, he or she works and works to control situations to make things okay.

A person who reacts with escape comes to a different conclusion. He or she usually thinks, *There is* nothing *I can do to make sure I am safe and know who I am.*

It is as if the escaper is completely overwhelmed by circumstances or feelings and comes to the conclusion the only thing to do is to get away.

While controllers react with power and often are in the fight reaction, escapers react in flight and disappear. Often they will disappear physically by going away and retreating to another setting, activity, or solitary place. But just as often, they will disappear emotionally by disconnecting from important relationships, hiding out with some kind of substance like drugs or alcohol, or even cognitively disassociating from reality. Some of the telltale characteristics that we see in an escaper's reactivity are numbing out emotionally, being addicted to an activity or substance, and being impulsive, dramatic, avoidant, or secretive.

This kind of disconnection does not bode well for reliability and responsibility. A person who escapes does not simply withdraw; he or she checks out totally from the situation. As a result, it is just a matter of time before the lack of attention to life and relationship shows up in irresponsibility and chaos.

Most people who react with escape have deep feelings that are tied to feeling unsafe, particularly when it comes to their abilities to take initiative, act in their own best interests, or have some empowerment in a situation. In short, many times the person mired in escape feels powerless or helpless and overwhelmed by the reality of life.

Almost all of us can relate to this reactivity at least a little. Those of us who escape in marginal ways may do it by eating too much, spending too much money, or sleeping too much. These are simple ways for us to escape the pressures of the everyday. But many of us get more serious about our escape reactions: we may drink or take drugs too much, watch porn too much, or gamble too much. In worst-case scenarios, people disassociate and have a mental break with reality. In these cases, individuals can have blocks of time where they are not aware of what they do or where they have been for hours and sometimes days at a time. In other situations, people disassociate into other variants of personality.

We often see this kind of reactivity associated with trauma due to war, criminal behavior, natural disaster, or disturbing relationships. No matter the cause or the severity of escape, however, it is important to realize that disconnection is bad for us as individuals and certainly is bad for relationships. Escapers are often secretive to protect themselves, and because they use substances or behaviors to anesthetize pain, they can be particularly prone to addictions.

Now for a bit of bad news. You can be reactive in one, two, three, or even all four of these ways—blame, shame, control, and escape. A few of us react predictably in a single way. Others of us react in multiple fight and flight manners, but even then the sequence is still usually somewhat predictable. For instance, in the next illustrations you will see Terry's and Sharon's primary emotions and their reactive coping.

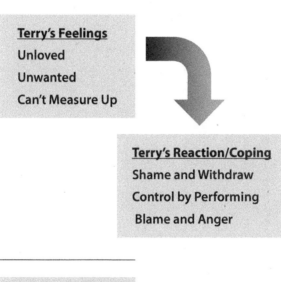

Terry's Feelings
Unloved
Unwanted
Can't Measure Up

Terry's Reaction/Coping
Shame and Withdraw
Control by Performing
Blame and Anger

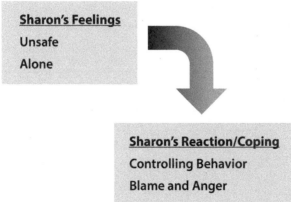

Sharon's Feelings
Unsafe
Alone

Sharon's Reaction/Coping
Controlling Behavior
Blame and Anger

As we have said before, many of us confuse our reactivity with our primary emotions. They are not the same. For example, in the illustrations above, you can see that both of us have anger—but we deal with our anger differently.

It is common enough for people to say, "I *feel* angry." But if you just stick with the feeling of anger, you miss the core of the issue and the energy that is driving the anger. For Terry, in the cycle above, the feeling that drives the reactivity of anger is *Can't measure up*. For Sharon, the reactivity of anger is driven by the feeling that she is unsafe and cannot effect a different outcome.

Now it is your turn to rightly reckon with yourself and identify the reactivity that is driven by the primary emotions you feel. Remember not to be hard on yourself and start thinking how "bad" or "destructive" you are in relationships. As you work through the next exercise, remember that you reacted in these ways because your brain is wired to a fight or flight response and you learned these things little by little over a long period of time.

EXERCISE 4
Identifying Your Normal Reactions

1. Look back at the feelings that you identified in Exercise 3, page 28. Write down these words below so you can remember them easily.

_____

_____

2. Now look at the list of words below that describe different reactions or coping behaviors. When you are feeling the primary emotions that you have written down in Question 1, how do you normally react? Circle two to five reactions or coping behaviors that best describe what you do.

Blames Others	Shames Self	Controls	Escapes/Creates Chaos
Rage	Depressed	Perfectionistic	Impulsive
Angry	Negative	Performs	Numbs Out
Sarcastic	Whines	Judgmental	Avoids Issues
Arrogant	Inconsolable	Demanding	Escapes Using Substance
Aggressive	Catastrophizing	Critical	Escapes Using Activity
Retaliatory	Manipulative	Defensive	Irresponsible
Threatening	Fearful	Anxious	Selfish
Punishing	Pouting	Intellectualizes	Minimizes
Fault Finding	Harms Self	Nagging	Addicted
Discouraging	Needy	Lecturing	Secretive

3. Take a few moments and consider the words that you have circled above. Are there any reactions that you would say describe what you do that are not listed above? Is so, write these additional words below.

_____

_____

Rightly Reckoning Part Two

Chances are, when you look at the words that you circled above in terms of your reactivity and coping, it looks pretty ugly to you. Also, somewhere inside your soul, you know you have repeated this cycle above with the feelings and reactivity again and again in your life and relationships. This is again how the brain works. Whenever we find these violations of love and trustworthiness and they have a damaging effect on our sense of identity and safety, we start constructing a habitual form of reacting that we turn to over and over. In fact, the reactions to the primary emotions come so quickly and so effortlessly that they appear to be automatic. For example, when I feel like my friend simply will not connect with me, I will find myself acting manipulative, angry, or depressed *even before I realize that I feel alone.* This is a testimony to just how fast the brain uses prior knowledge and makes the connections between primary emotions and our reactivity or coping.

One of the lessons we have learned from recent neuroscience discoveries is that the brain prefers neural pathways it already knows. In other words, what you have done and felt in the past sets up the preferred way your brain will chose to think and feel today. All of these connections, feelings, and coping reactions you find above are quite practiced and your brain considers these pathways most natural.

But if we are to reckon with ourselves rightly, we need to not only identify these reactions that are part of us and appear ugly but also realize that they are sinful and damaging.

First, they are damaging to us as people, since the reactions are a part of our worst and corrupted selves. James tells us that we need to find the locus of evil inside ourselves: "Let no one say when he is tempted, 'I am being tempted by God,' for God cannot be tempted with evil, and he himself tempts no one. But each person is tempted when he is lured and enticed by his own desire. Then desire when it has conceived gives birth to sin, and sin when it is fully grown brings forth death" (*James 1:13-15*). Your reactivity is quite understandable because you started the behaviors when you felt unsure of your identity or safety. But the fact is that, as you have practiced these behaviors, they have separated you further and further from the peace, love, and hope that God desires for you.

Second, this reactivity is extraordinarily damaging to the people who experience you in relationships. When you think about it, everything you do in terms of blame, shame, control, and escape is a violation of love and trustworthiness in other relationships. Another way of saying this is that there is *nothing* good that comes from reactivity of blame, shame, control, or escape. To prove this point, we only need to look as far as how people in our relationships react to us when we are at our worst.

Several years ago, when our son was nine, our house needed painting. At the time, I (Terry) was struggling with some physical issues that caused me to have joint pain and fatigue. But when the condition of the house worsened, I reasoned that I had to power through and simply get it done. It was a clear indication that I felt I should be able to do this "man's job," and I was full blown into performing.

One day, my nine year old came out to help and was excited to learn how to paint. I tried to be patient, but the truth was, I was over-focused on the job to be done and not focused at all upon sharing with and teaching my son. I showed him a few things and left him to work on his own while I did what I saw as the important work. As you would expect, he made some mistakes and ended up getting a good deal of paint on the brick, where it did not belong.

All he wanted to do was to help and spend time with me doing "man's work." But when I realized I was going to lose more time cleaning up his mess and have less energy in an already shrinking supply, I felt the full impact of the reality that I was failing at the job of painting the house. I wasn't measuring up. And as I felt the impact of my failure, I blew up at my son. I told him how incompetent he was and how he caused me to lose time and more energy. I inflicted his heart in every way I could to tell him that *he was now a failure.*

How did he react? In just the way you would expect of a fragile boy who put his heart in his father's hands, only to have it crushed. He shamed himself terribly, saying that he could not do anything right, and gave up. He withdrew and isolated himself. He also felt angry that I had treated him in such an unfair way. After all, he was only trying to help me. As you see in the next illustration, it was the perfect repeat of a painful cycle.

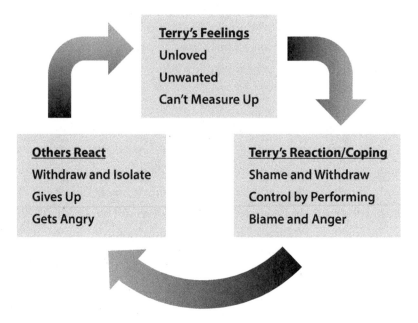

I thought I was painting the house, but in actuality I was shaping my son's heart. I did substantial damage to his confidence, identity, and sense of safety with me.

Notice that his reaction to me set the stage for my primary emotions to be triggered again. When he withdrew, gave up, and carried anger, I became more likely to feel unloved, unwanted, and like a failure who cannot measure up as a father. When triggered, I reacted and coped by going into my same old cycle of withdrawing and shaming myself, trying to perform my way out of these horrible feelings and setting the stage for more anger.

EXERCISE 5
Identifying Your Pain Cycle

1. Look back at the feelings that you identified in Exercise 3, page 28, and write down these words in the box marked "Feelings."

2. Look back at the reactivity or coping you identified in Exercise 4, page 39, and write down these words in the box marked "Reactivity/ Coping."

3. Think about how others behave or react to you consistently when you do what you do in your reactivity and coping. Write these reactions down in the box marked "Others React."

Feelings

1. _____
2. _____
3. _____
4. _____
5. _____

Others React

1. _____
2. _____
3. _____
4. _____
5. _____

Reactivity/Coping

1. _____
2. _____
3. _____
4. _____
5. _____

It is important to realize that our Pain Cycles have been repeated thousands of times whenever we get emotionally disregulated. In Terry's case, it was not painting the house or how he felt on that particular day that initiated the Pain Cycle for the first time. The situation merely triggered a Pain Cycle that had been inside him for a long time. Just like all of us, he repeats his Pain Cycle in relationships with other family members, his spouse, his co-workers, his friends, and his supervisors.

In many ways, this Pain Cycle you have just completed is the heart of the dragon—the heart of the issue behind all of your continuing issues of identity and safety.

A Tough Day of Reckoning

Day 1 of changing is always tough. Today you have had the courage to think about how your story of identity and safety have been woven together. You have organized this reality into identifying your primary emotions that drive the bulk of your fight or flight reactivity. Then you took the giant leap of understanding how these emotions drive you into some unloving and untrustworthy behaviors of your own by identifying your reactivity under the headings of blame, shame, control, and escape.

In one way, digging out all of this emotion and reckoning with the responsibility of the destructive things we do can be discouraging and exhausting. We would point you to two facts to encourage you.

First, you are not alone. All of us deal with the same kinds of feelings and reactions. For example, the apostle Paul said, "I know that nothing good dwells in me, that is, in my flesh. For I have the desire to do what is right, but not the ability to carry it out. For I do not do the good I want, but the evil I do not want is what I keep on doing" (*Romans 7:18-19*). Even Paul struggled with the reality of a Pain Cycle and found himself repeating the same pattern again and again.

The encouraging second point is that you now understand the cycle in such a way that you can get a different kind of leverage on the problem of doing what you desire not to repeat. In the next chapter you will find that there is a way to start the process of changing these old and sinful patterns that exist in your Pain Cycle.

For Reflection

Note: If you are working in a small group, you might consider taking two group meetings to go over the following material so you have time to hear each person's response.

1. Discuss with a friend or a group what you think the most powerful influences were in your life in terms of your identity formation or your beliefs about relationships and safety.

2. Talk about your Pain Cycle with a friend or a group, being sure to identify the primary emotions or what you feel when you get emotionally disregulated and what you do in your coping or reactivity.

3. Recount out loud the story of the last time you were emotionally disregulated or the last conflict you had with someone. Have a friend or a group help you identify what you felt and did during that time. Did you find that it confirmed or disconfirmed the Pain Cycle? Remember that the point of the exercise is to understand yourself, not to comment on the behavior of the other person in the conflict.

4. Read again James 1:13-15: "Let no one say when he is tempted, 'I am being tempted by God,' for God cannot be tempted with evil, and he himself tempts no one. But each person is tempted when he is lured and enticed by his own desire. Then desire when it has conceived gives birth to sin, and sin when it is fully grown brings forth death." In thinking about this passage, your own background, and what you know about God, what sense do you make of your Pain Cycle? What can you learn from your Pain Cycle? Knowing your Pain Cycle, what steps would you like to take next in your growth and learning?

DAY TWO

— ♦ ♦ —

Confronting the Lies and Telling Truth

Although we did not know him well, the profound writer and Catholic priest Henri Nouwen stepped into our lives at exactly the right time to give us a precious gift. Terry was struggling with a bout of clinical depression. Like all depression, it came on him when he did not want it and would not go away when he told it to. We were taking care of an aging parent and learning to find ourselves in our careers, but otherwise nothing tragic was going on in our lives. Still, depression hung over him like a toxic plume over a volcano.

Henri also struggled with depression for a good portion of his life. He was deeply spiritual, very successful, and committed to loving and doing well for others. Yet the dark cloud also hung over him. On a visit with Terry, Henri said, "You keep waiting and praying for the depression to lift as if it is a circumstance that will change. You will have to eventually change your perspective and ask yourself the question, how will I live my life if the depression never lifts and nothing in life changes?" For us, it was a game changer in the way we viewed life.

We all have internal messages about our basic identity and our sense of safety. Our histories up to this point have already been written, and there is little or nothing we can do to rewrite the past. The reality we face is that, when we find our new self, it must overlay or coexist with much of the muck we cannot change. Like Terry's depression, we can hope it goes away on its own, but at some point we have to recognize that the right question is, how will I live my life if these struggles over my identity and sense of safety persist?

How do we live life with Pain Cycles that have repeated themselves thousands of times and will likely keep raising their heads to be repeated in the future? How do we live life in such a way that we experience what Paul was pointing to when he spoke about the love of Christ? "In all these things we are more than conquerors through him who loved us" (*Romans 8:37*).

You are More Powerful than You Think

One of the amazing things about humans is that we are a complex version of all our development. It is like we come into life with an efficiency apartment of one room—uncomplicated and easy to clean. As we grow and develop, we add on more and more rooms, closets, and halls. By the time we reach late adolescence and early adulthood, we have a complex labyrinth of rooms upon more rooms that stick together like a maze. So it is with our development: we all carry with us original programming and ideas about our identity and sense of safety. These ideas were modified and we were given different messages along the way, but we still carry the original development and conclusions we came to, particularly when those early ideas and development involved some type of injury.

For many of us, the most powerful messages about our identity and sense of safety came from our parents, caregivers, and families. This makes sense, as they were, in most cases, the original programmers of love and trustworthiness for us, and so our early development latched on firmly to these ideas.

For others of us, we have little qualms with the way our families raised us, even though they were not perfect. As we mentioned before, however, in our later development we were challenged by peers, teachers, or mentors who left us feeling far from loved and safe.

I (Terry) am slightly dyslectic. I struggled in my early years with understanding and comprehending reading. Once, in second grade, I was given a grammar assignment involving ten sentences containing blanks where we were supposed to fill in the proper use of *have, has,* or *had.* I did not understand the assignment. My teacher took time to explain it to me, but that did not help me. My mother explained it to me later, but I was still lost. When my father tried to help, I just could not get the concept, and out of his frustration he said, "Terry, the word must fit the sentence."

Magic. Immediately I had all I needed to properly understand grammar.

"The word must fit the sentence." I took out a ruler and measured the blanks and then painstakingly matched the words have, has, and had based on size. Grammar was easy!

It was easy until I took the assignment to my teacher and she questioned how I came up with such answers. I gladly explained to her how easy grammar was if people had good rulers.

I still remember the dumbfounded look on my teacher's face at the end of my story. Maybe she was having a bad day, but if I'm remembering correctly, she said, "Terry, you are so dumb."

I latched on to the pronouncement and believed it down to my very soul. Intellectually, I was lacking. Because I believed I was dumb, I carried the words with me through my academic career. I developed further, but the belief that I was dumb was programmed in from then on throughout my high school years.

In other words, the programming about our identity and sense of safety does not have to come from family in order to be powerful; it can also come from friends, former spouses, teachers and coaches, or anyone else who made a powerful impact on our development. As we mentioned before when talking about Sharon's history, it can also come from traumatic events over which we had little or no control.

However we have developed these perspectives on ourselves and our relationships, the ideas get set dramatically and reliably into our development, and no matter how many rooms we add on, we tend to go back to those powerful and, most often, early developmental rooms. We treat these messages as unchangeable and static. It is almost as if we reason, *Since this message came from my parents (or my teachers, friends, my mentors, or early life experience), it must be true.* But it is not. It is actually a lie.

For several reasons, we do not challenge false beliefs.

First, we do not challenge these beliefs because many of us have never taken the time to identify the feelings associated with being loved and feeling safe. We get trapped by our escape mechanisms, shame, blame, control, and withdrawal and never trace back to the primary emotions we feel that are driving our destructive behaviors. Then, once the destructive behavior occurs, we secretly think it confirms our lies about ourselves.

Second, many of us don't challenge beliefs about our identity and sense of safety because we believe it is someone else's job to do so. We want our parents to make it right with us or prove to us that we are important, special, and worthy. Others of us want God to take away our faulty outlooks in our identity and confirm in us a love and trustworthiness so powerful that they drive all self-doubt away. Most of us want others to take responsibility to convince us about something different regarding identity and safety.

Finally, and often most true, many of us have never considered the possibility that we have the power to speak into ourselves about our identity and sense of safety. It simply does not register on us that we are not powerless in this area and that, somewhere in the process of becoming an adult, we gained the authority and capability of making a difference in our own programming.

We remember well, as adults in our twenties, thirties, and even forties, walking into situations with our families where we somehow assumed that the original message programmed into us was still the message we had to accept. For instance, Terry assumed well into his thirties that unless his mother and father approved of his choices, he was somehow a failure. Sharon assumed well into adulthood that if she disagreed with her mother and it resulted in confrontation, it would disrupt harmony and peace in her group, making it unsafe.

In his lovely book *Life of the Beloved*, Henri Nouwen speaks about the responsibility that each of us carries in confronting faulty identity and safety. Nouwen says we must be willing to do three things: (1) confront and reject the lie; (2) tell ourselves and embrace the truth; and (3) engage others who will tell us the truth.[2]

Such simple but sound advice.

We want you to realize that you are much more powerful than you think and you have some ability to confront the message and original programming you received. You are not a powerless child without any control over your life. You may not have had this power when you originally received the message about identity or safety, but you are not age three, eight, or even eighteen anymore. You have power to confront the lie and embrace the truth.

In a different context, the writer of Hebrews talks about growing up and learning to think in a more mature way: "Though by this time you ought to be teachers, you need someone to teach you again the basic principles of the oracles of God. You need milk, not solid food, for everyone who lives on milk is unskilled in the work of righteousness, since he is a child. But solid food is for the mature, for those who have their powers of discernment trained by constant practice to distinguish good from evil" (*Hebrews 5:12-14*). With this perspective in mind, it is time to acknowledge that, even though as a child you may not have had the power to effect changes in your identity or sense of safety, you are no longer trapped. You have the wisdom, power, and strength to confront past lies about your identity and safety.

Sources of the Truth: Self, God and Others

It should not be a surprise that you are powerful in terms of taking responsibility for your identity and sense of safety. Many times, we find that Christians have the expectation that God should take away all struggles and self-doubts as well as put up a shield of protection to make us immune to unsafe situation. Yet it is clear that we are given responsibility and power to chose not only what we do but also what we think. Consider these verses that talk about our choice to cooperate with the Holy Spirit in our thinking and doing:

> "Those who live according to the flesh set their minds on the things
> of the flesh, but those who live according to the Spirit set their minds on
> the things of the Spirit. For to set the mind on the flesh is death, but to
> set the mind on the Spirit is life and peace." (*Romans 8:5-6*)

"I say, walk by the Spirit, and you will not gratify the desires of the flesh." (*Galatians 5:16*)

We have a choice to walk in the ways of the flesh or to walk in the ways of the Spirit. God seems committed not to overcome our power to choose. In this sense and on this issue, God makes us more powerful than even His own being.

In our practices with clients, we consistently find it true that people willfully reject the truth. People have others who tell them sincerely, "I love you and I see how precious you are." Yet these same people often reject what others say and root themselves in a belief that they are alone, unloved, and have nothing special about their beings. Likewise, we see folks read inspiring Bible passages about how God loves them and how God will never leave them alone, only to proclaim that the words are either unbelievable or do not apply to them.

God will not take away the power of the individual to choose either "the things of the flesh" or "the things of the Spirit"—the way of lies or the way of truth. The self, therefore, is the most powerful source of truth for the individual. If we choose not to speak the truth about ourselves, then neither God nor any other person is going to overcome that decision.

Confront and reject the lie.

If we buy into the idea that we have the power and responsibility to speak life and truth into ourselves, how do we go about the task?

Remember the first point of Nouwen's perspective: we must confront and reject the lie. We do this in a powerful way by first doing the work that you did in the Day 1 chapter. By organizing the framework to identify the primary emotions you feel concerning identity and safety, you take a giant step in knowing the core of the issue you must confront and kill.

Sharon grew up in an environment where half the members of her family were taken by sudden and tragic means. Terry grew up in a family that had destructive and hurtful patterns and he was isolated. Was it true that Sharon was perpetually unsafe and that Terry was unloved? That is certainly what we felt, but it did not represent the truth about relationships and who we were as people. But the organization of the Pain Cycle helps us to name and confront the lie.

One of the pastors in our church, Mark Pickrell, confidently states, "You cannot change what you will not name." Sharon feels chronically unsafe and I chronically feel unloved. Until we name the lie that we were taught or came to believe, we have little hope of claiming a truth that will address it and eventually make life different.

Organizing your brain by using the Pain Cycle and understanding this fact represents not only your pain but also your holding on to the things of the flesh helps you get the leverage you need to confront the lie about your identity and sense of safety. It allows you to objectively look at the perspective of your pain in definable terms and decide whether or not the words describing the primary emotions are true or false.

For instance, was Terry really dumb when he did not understand the grammar exercise in second grade? Of course not. Terry had limitations in terms of learning, but Terry is not dumb. Was he unloved or was he unlovable in his family? Absolutely not. His parents made some unfortunate choices due to their own backgrounds of physical abuse and their own limitations of pain concerning their identity and sense of safety, but they were not unloving people and neither were they making a commentary that Terry was unlovable.

Was Sharon unsafe and abandoned to be alone? While the world can be an unsafe place at times, it does not mean that the world is out of control and that relationships cannot work for good. Certainly, the unsafe situation does not mean that Sharon is alone. She was separated from half of her family by death, but she also had faithful and loyal people around her to stand with her in times of need. Sharon's safety is not total, but it is present and she certainly is not alone.

Looking at your Pain Cycle and confronting the lie by examining the primary emotions will help you move toward eventual change.

EXERCISE 6
Evaluating Your Primary Emotions

1. Look back at the Pain Cycle you described in Exercise 5, page 43. Pay particular attention to the primary emotions you listed in the "Feelings" box.

2. What you feel is what you feel. But regardless of how you came by that primary emotion (through the actions of family members, mentors, coaches, peers, or situations or trauma), how do the feelings misrepresent the truth or reality about your identity or the safety of relationships?

3. If the feelings misrepresent the truth or reality about your identity or about relationships (particularly current relationships), what are the reasons, circumstances, situations, limitations, and developmental history behind your ending up with these feelings? Write some of these reasons behind the lies down below.

_____

_____

Tell yourself and embrace the truth

It is fair to wonder how we come to believe anything as the truth about who we are as individuals and how relationships work. Mostly, we come to adopt ideas as truth because we accommodate what someone else has taught us in our brains. We mostly do not analyze and systematically go about a process of scientific inquiry to determine truth. For almost all of us, lies or truth both are taught to us by our experiences and relationships. In other words, our beliefs about identity and relational safety are woven together by the story of our lives. If we are exposed to a story long enough, we tend to believe that is the way the story *should* go is how we have heard it before.

One might wonder, therefore, how we determine if anything is true. It is enough for us to sometimes throw up our hands and assume that the postmodern philosophical tenet that *there is no truth but only constructed ideas* is the correct assumption. When we are speaking about telling ourselves and embracing the truth in this context, we are actually combining the two realities that there are foundational truths that we can hold on to and that we need to engage a narrative or experience that gives us a chance to interpret identity and safety differently.

The foundational truths that we would maintain are real are these: (1) human beings are valuable and important; and (2) relationships are essential and should promote human growth. It would be easy to maintain these truths from the perspective of the Bible, which we will do later, but here we want to take the perspective of why these things are true and practicable even apart from the Bible.

First, human beings are valuable and important because we are the most evolved species and stand at the pinnacle of reason and power. We also regularly put the interests of others above our own interests. We believe that all people— weak, old, poor, uneducated, powerful, young, rich, educated—should not only survive but also thrive. This concept exists almost nowhere else in the animal kingdom. Even apart from Christianity, we embrace the truth that humans are valuable and important.

Second, there is a truth that relationships are essential and are built to promote growth. One way we would maintain that this is a fundamental truth is that humans have no way of knowing themselves or shaping identity apart from relationships with others. Imagine if an infant or toddler was never exposed to the love, bonding, and warmth of another human being. We actually know that in cases of extreme neglect or limitation the child who is denied relationship with a caregiver suffers from severe developmental delay and may fail to thrive, even to the point of death. Everything we know about ourselves and everything we learn about functioning in the world is built around the dependence on relationships. If we do not experience relationship, then we simply do not know who we are and we not only fail to develop socially but also fail to develop emotionally, physically, and cognitively. Like it or not, humans are built for relationships and cannot grow successfully or normally without them. This is true because it is a fundamental reality of life proven by long and systematic observation.

If you would agree that these two propositions are true, then the next question to consider is, what do I choose to believe about myself and about relationships? We all come from a background where we have faulty ideas about our identity and have doubts about our sense of safety in relationships. We have confronted these lies where we were not treated as valuable and important human beings and where others did not care for us in ways that were safe and helped us grow. But now it is time to take that mature and adult position on ourselves and decide what truth we will believe. Continuing to believe the lies about our identity or safety will land us right back in the Pain Cycle. In order to yield something different in our identity and sense of safety, we must learn to embrace an *emotionally regulating truth* into our story and our experience.

One way that we learn to embrace this emotionally regulating truth is to use imagery called *reparenting*. In reparenting, we see ourselves at the age and in the circumstance where we received the injury. For example, Sharon might imagine herself as the thirteen-year-old girl who was devastated after learning of her brother's murder. Terry might concentrate on a particularly difficult time when he was eight years old and was feeling the height of incompetency and isolation in his family. When we mentally go back to these times, we imagine that we see and hear what was going on and feel the emotions our younger selves felt during these harsh and trying times. We do not, however, see ourselves as if we were them; we see our younger selves from our perspective as an adult. We see them as if we were watching them on a screen or speaking to them from our perspective in the here and now. We know how we felt in the images we see. We ask ourselves, "What truth do I want to share with this image of myself that addresses how he (or she) feels?"

This is a big step and can be quite emotional. We recommend that you do not just think your way through the exercise but you say out loud the truths and words you would say about the identity and sense of safety you felt at that time. We say this for two reasons. First, saying the words out loud ensures that you will likely stay in your adult or mature self and speak to the younger or injured you as a loving and caring parent. And second, it increases the possibility that you will actually have an emotional experience of the truth being spoken and challenging the lies and feelings that you normally have regarding identity and safety.

We are not trying to make you feel emotional for no particular reason. We know that when we feel emotions in the here and now, it actually is a sign that the brain is taking in the experience in a more impactful manner. You are speaking and emotionally regulating truth to yourself for the purpose of teaching your brain to embrace the truth rather than the feelings that are regularly triggered by your identity and sense of safety.

There are, of course, variations that you can do on the above imagery. For instance, we have individuals who, after seeing images of themselves as vulnerable and hurt, write letters or short messages from the parental perspective. This is a great adaptation, and if you want to try it, we suggest that after you write the letter or message, you read the word aloud to make the experience as real as possible. Some also use their creativity in this exercise by writing a song or poem of truth. Others compile computer-generated pictures of themselves when they were younger and as they are now to demonstrate the adult perspective they take. Still others go to a special spot where they remember feeling the most vulnerable about identity and safety. No matter how you chose to implement the work, it is essential that you take the perspective that you are a powerful parent of yourself and that you are now deciding the truth that you choose to tell yourself about your identity and sense of safety.

Most of us, when we confront the reality of the image of ourselves at emotionally vulnerable times and places can garner the courage and maturity to say the right things from an adult perspective. But how about now? Can you extend the work you do on the truth to reparent yourself at those emotionally vulnerable times long ago to parenting yourself when those emotions are triggered in the here and now? Part of the challenge of taking responsibility to tell yourself and embrace the truth is to, not only look at yourself when you originally felt the pain of identity and safety, but also look at yourself in those times in the here and now when you have those old messages triggered. Look at yourself in the mirror or look at a current picture of yourself. This person also needs to hear the truth from you concerning his or her identity and sense of safety. Can you say the same reassuring truths to your adult self in the here and now that you did when you were younger and more vulnerable?

EXERCISE 7
Reliving Your Pain Cycle in Operation

1. Think about a time and place where you felt the pain of identity or safety that is reflected in your Pain Cycle. How old were you? How did you look at this age? If you're comfortable with it, look at yourself at this time when you were vulnerable in your pain as if you were seeing it on a movie screen. Note how this version you are seeing feels in terms of love and trust-worthiness.

2. If you were speaking directly to the feelings of this version of you, knowing how he or she struggles with identity and safety, what is it you would want to say concerning the truth about his or her personhood or safety in relationships? Remember to speak these words out loud and from a position of a mature parent who wants to help the vulnerable image to understand the truth about his or her value and the importance of security in relationships.

3. Record the words you said or a few of the ideas you shared with the vulnerable image of yourself.

_____

_____

_____

It is so necessary to speak the truth about identity and safety in relationships because pain originates from the lies we have believed about these two issues. We did not just feel this pain once, but as we have stated before, we have felt this pain over and over again because our brains are most sensitized to the threats.

EXERCISE 8
Identifying Your Emotionally Regulating Truths

1. As you think about emotionally regulating the painful lies about your identity and sense of safety, what are the words below that are meaningful and powerful to you? Circle three to five words that you would like to be able to claim as your own to represent the new reality about your identity and sense of safety.

Loved	Adequate	Safe	Protected
Worthy	Approved	Secure	Connected
Significant	Accepted	Sure	Intimate
Not alone	Wanted	Fulfilled	Competent
Prized	Appreciated	Capable	Validated
Valuable	Hopeful	Empowered	Successful
Precious	Free	In control	Enough

2. In looking at the words you have circled above, are there slight changes you can make that would make the truths more of your own? Or are there different words that would make more sense to you? Write these thoughts, changes, or words down below.

_____

3. Take a few moments and list the words you have circled and identified in the box on page 60. Try to include just the most important words that you wish to include as your truths and that have the power to regulate your identity and safety in relationships.

Truths
1. _____
2. _____
3. _____
4. _____
5. _____

Hopefully you are able to identify some of the truths that would correct the lies that you were taught about your identity and sense of safety. In the next exercise, you can consolidate, organize, and structure some of those truths into a package of emotionally regulating words that make a difference when you feel pain or are triggered in your Pain Cycle.

Safety is Tricky

One more thing about the truth about safety: it is tricky.

Most of us would readily agree that individuals are valuable and deserving of love. It is much more difficult to come to the conclusion that the world is a safe place…because it is *not* safe. The interstate highway that I try to cross on foot does not magically turn into a sidewalk in order to protect me. Likewise, when I am in relationship with dangerous people, they do not suddenly become trustworthy, and there may be nobody else to protect me. At times, neither the physical world nor the emotional world of relationships is safe.

So, what kind of truth can we tell ourselves and embrace when we are emotionally disregulated on this fact of safety?

First, while we are not totally safe, we are far from totally *unsafe.* The reality is that we are empowered to make certain choices that make us much safer.

For example, although no one can guarantee that I will be safe in my home or neighborhood, I can take steps to increase my power and the likelihood that I will be kept safe. I can be attentive to the people around me and the things that go on in my neighborhood and take responsibility to make sure regular patrols take place and that gang signals and discarded items are promptly removed. When I go for a walk or step out to the garage, I can make sure that I am not alone or that I am in areas that are well lighted. I can pay attention and implement good security practices in my home. Am I totally safe and protected? Of course not. But I am empowered to take actions that can achieve a good and tolerable degree of safety.

Human empowerment is essential if we are going to stabilize situations.

Inmates of concentration camps during World War II had seemingly every bit of power taken from them and were in an environment that was certainly unsafe. Yet a survivor of one of these camps told about how most of his fellow survivors hid small strips of cloth on their persons. At the end of the day, when they were given a meager cup of watered-down soup, the survivors would drink all but a swallow. With the remaining liquid, they would soak the strip of cloth and wash. One of the survivors insisted that if one stopped washing, they would give up and die.[3]

Here were people who were in control of nothing, yet they found hope in a small strip of cloth and the ritual of washing. This deep level of empowerment in the face of an unsafe world should remind us all that we have the power to affect our own circumstances. While our power cannot ensure safety, we can make choices that move us toward stability and structure.

Second, recognizing that the world is not safe can do us some good. Most people can point to difficult times or circumstances in their lives as teaching them lessons or growing them up in ways that they would have never have chosen if they were going to keep themselves safe.

For instance, one of our friends who joined the Marines spoke about the tremendous impact it had on his life. "I hated almost every part of my first three months in the Marines," he said, "but it taught me something I never forgot. It taught me that there are few things I cannot be successful at if I am willing to keep going and I am not concerned who gets the credit."

Hard times and difficult circumstances shape us in ways that make us grow in character and virtue. Things may look unsafe, but they may also teach us essential information.

Still, some things don't make sense and can't be considered safe or good. We need to consider these things from a perspective of the long haul. For instance, it looks to us as if Sharon's father's suicide created an unsafe situation for her when she was growing up. But her father's suicide also created a scenario where Sharon's family packed up and moved from California to Texas. Around the same time, Terry's parents lost everything they had in a farming failure and moved to Texas to find work. Ten years later, we met and eventually married, producing two wonderful children.

Now, was it a good or safe thing that Sharon's father committed suicide and Terry's parents went bankrupt? Certainly not. But unsafe and bad things can lead to safe, secure, and good things.

Would we have ended up married had not these unsafe and tragic things occurred? Perhaps. But it is easy to see how unsafe tragedy led to a safe harbor for us. As Christians, we know this promise well: "All things work together for good, for those who are called according to his purpose" (*Romans 8:28*). The promise does not state that all things are good but that all things work together for good. In the end, we have to realize that the truth about an unsafe world is that even tragic times and circumstances can lead us to necessary growth and eventual safe harbor.

Engage others who tell you the truth.

We love this quote from Maya Angelou: "Courage is the most important of all of the virtues, because without courage you can't practice any other virtue consistently. You can practice any virtue erratically, but nothing consistently without courage."[4] For instance, without courage you will never be able to achieve the openness required in honesty or the consistent commitment to connection and love required in compassion.

Courage—the virtue of commitment to keep moving forward even though your brain tells you a different message of fear—is the key to accomplishing great change. This was the case when Joshua led the people of Israel to the edge of the Promised Land, where they were to cross the Jordan River. The people had been in this place forty years before when Moses was the leader. But back then, there had been a big problem. From their perspective, the obstacles were too great and their enemies were too big and powerful. But this time, a word came to the people from God through Joshua: "Be strong and courageous, for you shall cause this people to inherit the land that I swore to their fathers to give them. Only be strong and very courageous, being careful to do according to all the law that Moses my servant commanded you. Do not turn from it to the right hand or to the left, that you may have good success wherever you go" (*Joshua 1:6-7*).

You have been in this place before also. You have heard the good words and truth about your identity from God and many other people before. Indeed, you have had encouragement from God and others that you are more powerful and gifted than you think in confronting a difficult world. You have been in the place before where others and God have assured you that they are with you and they have your back. It is right to reckon with yourself that, at this time and place in your life, you will either claim these truths about your identity and sense of safety for yourself or you will not. God and other people will not be able to override the message that you insist on believing. You are at the edge of confronting the most basic of feelings about yourself and how those primary emotions give rise to all sorts of unloving and untrustworthy reactions toward yourself and others. You must have courage to make the decision to claim the regulating truth for yourself. No one else can do this job for you. This is the reality of what you have done in (1) confronting and rejecting the lie and (2) telling yourself and embracing the truth.

But courage does not mean you accomplish the task all in one giant leap. It is done—just as it was done with the children of Israel entering the Promised Land—one step, one mile, one city, one region at a time. You will have times when you falter and have difficulty. To have courage means that you keep going and remain resolute to move forward instead of retreating into the mindset of the old feelings and lies you tell yourself about your identity and relationships. If you have courage, it opens the pathway for you to eventually find the truth about who you are and about relationships.

If you have the courage to claim and believe the truth about yourself, then it starts to make a difference to engage others who will also tell you the truth. God and others cannot do the work for you in terms of your responsibility of regulating past emotions, but they can do great things in encouraging you along the pathway. You must care for and reaffirm yourself, but you are not the only one who cares for and affirms your identity and work in relationships. Finding others who will affirm the truth in you is a tremendous encouragement to you to keep having the courage to do the right things.

God loves you. Most people, and particularly Christians, know this concept well intellectually but somehow forget the amazing grace that is involved with God's love. Here, as reminders and encouragement, we will point out just a few ways God loves you.

First, you were chosen by God. As Paul says, "He chose us in him before the foundation of the world, that we should be holy and blameless before him. In love he predestined us for adoption as sons through Jesus Christ, according to the purpose of his will" (*Ephesians 1:4-5*).

One of the things that is amazing about adoption in almost all cultures is that, under the law, once you are adopted, there is no differentiation between adopted and biological children. When children are biological, they are treasured and belong because they have the genetic markers of the parents. In adoption, the marker that the child is treasured and belongs is made by choice and proclamation. The first reason that we can point to that indicates that you are deeply loved is that God knew you before creation and intentionally made the choice to put the mark of adoption on you.

Second, you are loved because God made you for a particular purpose. Here again the apostle Paul states the truth: "We are his workmanship, created in Christ Jesus for good works, which God prepared beforehand, that we should walk in them" (*Ephesians 2:10*). In this verse, the idea of "workmanship" means that you were crafted like a fine piece of jewelry or a beautiful painting. You are a masterpiece in which God has taken time to make sure you have all the gifts, talents, and capabilities to do good work in relationships.

No one is quite like you in the way you were crafted by God, who makes you unique in personhood. This kind of meticulous craftsmanship reflects how much God cares about you and intends you to express that unique gift for the purpose of good.

Yet we know that, despite being loved by God through His choice of us and His craftsmanship in us, we have faltered and strayed from our God. Consider this devastating conclusion:

> "None is righteous, no, not one;
> no one understands;
> no one seeks for God.
> All have turned aside; together they have become worthless;
> no one does good,
> not even one."
> "Their throat is an open grave;
> they use their tongues to deceive."
> "The venom of asps is under their lips."
> "Their mouth is full of curses and bitterness."

"Their feet are swift to shed blood;
in their paths are ruin and misery,
and the way of peace they have not known."
"There is no fear of God before their eyes." (*Romans 3:10-18*)

Surely, as you read this passage, there is something in the list that applies to you as you have decided to follow your own ways of doing things and have forgotten about the way you were chosen and made.

As created beings, our rejection of the Creator is profound. But here we once again find the grace and love of God in that He wants us as we are and made great sacrifice to make sure that we have a way to stay connected in right relationship.

Consider the mix of failure and rescue: "All have sinned and fall short of the glory of God, and are justified by his grace as a gift, through the redemption that is in Christ Jesus, whom God put forward as a propitiation by his blood, to be received by faith. This was to show God's righteousness, because in his divine forbearance he had passed over former sins. It was to show his righteousness at the present time, so that he might be just and the justifier of the one who has faith in Jesus" (*Romans 3:23-26*).

Despite our falling short on so many counts, God wants us and makes great sacrifice on the part of Jesus to make sure that even in our sin we can and do belong to God. We have the mark that we are chosen. We are meticulously crafted for purpose. We are loved unconditionally and sacrificially. This fact should strengthen and encourage our identities that we are indeed unique and worthy.

God loves us like no other. But others also love us.

Earlier we discussed that, while none of us received perfect love and trustworthiness from our families, mentors, or caretakers, neither were there any situations where we were totally bereft of these elements. The reality is that, if we received no love or trustworthiness from anyone, we would not have survived and would have no sense of identity or relational safety. There were flaws in the way we were loved and held safe, but it does not negate the fact that others do care.

One way we know this is by the way others make sacrifices on our behalf.

Even while I was growing up in a difficult situation, my (Terry's) family and parents were consistently making sacrifices to make my life better. Both my mother and my father worked multiple jobs during my childhood to make sure we had a house and food. My parents often went without clothes and shoes for themselves to make sure my brothers, sister, and I had enough clothes to go to school and participate in activities.

If we are honest with ourselves, most of us will admit that we have had other people in our lives who extended themselves to make sure we knew we were loved. It may have been a teacher who took the extra time to mentor us or a coach who would not give up on us even when we were clearly not the best. It may have been a friend who sat with us for long hours just to make sure we were not alone in a tough time. Or it may have been some people we hardly knew who saw something in us that created hope, and so they put money toward our education or set opportunities in our path. In all of these situations, big or small, these others were weighing in on our identity.

It is easy to forget the truth about how we are loved and precious, especially when we are triggered by a long-standing program that tells us we are unloved, unwanted, unworthy, or below average and rejected as a failure. But if we are willing to begin the process of telling ourselves the truth about our identity, the words and actions of God and others begin to make a real difference in our lives in encouraging us to hold fast to the truth instead of the lies that are in the program.

We are not alone in the process of becoming our best selves. We are encouraged by our faith community.

The writer of Hebrews said, "Since we are surrounded by so great a cloud of witnesses, let us also lay aside every weight, and sin which clings so closely, and let us run with endurance the race that is set before us, looking to Jesus, the founder and perfecter of our faith, who for the joy that was set before him endured the cross, despising the shame, and is seated at the right hand of the throne of God" (*Hebrews 12:1-2*). So we have both living and passed-on saints rooting for us.

Imagine that you are on the field in a vast stadium filled with familiar faces and people down through the ages who now know intimately the love of God. This enormous crowd is chanting and doing the wave. In unison, they are shouting the truth about who you are and affirming your identity. Instead of "We're number one!" they are shouting things like "You are loved. No one is precious like you. Remember who you are!" All of them, living and past, are encouraging you to overcome your inner doubt and struggle and the hurdle of the programmed lie.

You are not alone. Engage others to tell you the truth about yourself and encourage you with the hope you need to take on a world and relationships that are not always safe.

Before we leave this imagery, we must find one more figure down on the field with us. Jesus—God in flesh—is there with us, encouraging us to overcome the lies that fill us with doubt about our identity and our ability to face uncertainty and lack of safety in the world. He is the most excellent of all encouragers and the best coach of all time. Why? Because He not only knows us well but also intimately knows the struggle we face.

Jesus faced constant persecution from leaders of His day who were telling Him that He was not who He knew He was and who were plotting to do Him harm. He was tempted to take easy ways out by proving who He was by His power instead of His love. He did not perform up to the world's expectations and often needed to withdraw at important times to regain connection and focus. He faced down the same temptations and doubts that you and I face. And at the end of His life, He faced the ultimate challenges of an unsafe world as He was completely deserted and went through indescribable pain and suffering and then died. Christ endured the betrayal, the trial, the beatings, the whip, the cross, the desertions, and finally death because He was firmly rooted in the knowledge that He was deeply loved and ultimately safe from all harm.

This is our mentor and coach out on the field. He knows our name and our every thought and weakness. Most of all, He knows the truth about us.

EXERCISE 9
Getting Help to Hear the Truth

1. Take a few moments and consider the truth that God would speak about your identity and safety in relationships. Give yourself about five minutes to listen to God and see if any of these messages about truth are confirmed in you. Perhaps you can hear something like Jesus heard when a voice from heaven said, "You are my beloved Son; with you I am well pleased' " (*Mark 1:11*). Write down some truths that you think God wants to speak about you and your safety.

_____

_____

2. Now think about the people on whom you regularly depend and who are faithful to stand by you in times of need or in times of joy. What words about your identity do these people regularly say to you? Write these words down and remember them as encouragement to the truth you have already identified.

_____

_____

3. All of us face hard times when we feel like we do not belong and we have no safety net. Think of the one, two, or three people you can depend on to always stand with you to ensure you are not alone even when the problems or pain cannot be solved. Make note of these people below.

_____

_____

4. Remember also that no matter what you face—inner struggles about your identity or overwhelming challenges from circumstances or relationships—Jesus is also there as a comforter, coach, and mentor. Think of a verse that affirms this reality for you and write it below.

_____

_____

No one can do this work for you, not even Jesus. You must be willing to confront the lies that you have believed about your identity and sense of safety and must claim the truth for yourself. But after you have done this work, you can find the encouragement to keep going in life by looking around you and noticing the friends, family, partners, and fellow followers of Jesus who affirm the reality of who you are and who will not leave you, because they understand the struggle. You will also find God, who is reminding you in the midst of struggles that you are not alone and you will never be deserted or forsaken.

A Day of Claiming Truth and Driving a Stake

In the old days, when pioneers set out to settle new places, they would search hard for just the right spot where they thought they could make a new life. They wanted a place that was not merely survivable but one where they and their families could thrive. When they had the "This is it!" moment, they drove stakes in the ground to mark off the boundary lines signifying that this is where they would make their new home.

On Day 2, you are doing that settling work in the territory of your brain where you are considering new ways to think about your identity and sense of safety in relationships. You have acclimated to the terrain of realizing that no one will do this work for you and you must have the courage to make statements to yourself, just as a parent would to a young child. In a real way, you have used this day to drive a stake in the ground of the new territory of claiming for yourself the identity and sense of behavior you want to have in relationships. You are the pioneer who has confronted the lies of the old way of thinking and have started the tough work of identifying and claiming the truth about your identity and safety.

You also have identified how to find community and partners who will agree with the new stakes you have set in the ground claiming the new territory. Furthermore, you have remembered that God also wants to tell you the truth you the truth about yourself and your relationships. You have internalized this promise: "I know the plans I have for you, declares the LORD, plans for welfare and not for evil, to give you a future and a hope" (*Jeremiah 29:11*). Your family, friends, partners, and God agree with the stakes you have driven in the ground to claim the territory of the new truth that will sink down and regulate the old primary emotions that have given you so much pain in your life and have prompted such strange coping and reactive behavior. It is the end of a new day.

Now that you have identified the truth where you want to live, it is time to get an accurate map of the territory you possess and start exploring how to live a new life in this place. The Pain Cycle will continue to be with you, but you will learn in the next chapter how to start implementing and mapping a new strategy based in peace.

For Reflection

1. This chapter teaches that the self is powerful in determining the truth one believes about his or her identity or sense of safety. What have you learned about the self being more powerful than others and God in influencing truth about identity and safety? Discuss some of your thoughts with a friend or a group.

2. Talk about your experiences in this chapter identifying elements of truth about your identity and sense of safety. Was it easier for you to identify truths from a list or to identify yourself as a parent talking to yourself? What truths did you identify? Share these thoughts, experiences, and truths with a friend or a group.

3. Talk with a friend or a group about the people who serve as encouragers to your sense of self and safety. If you were to narrow this down to just one person, how does he or she make a difference in your life and how do you feel after you spend time with him or her? Pay careful attention to how this person encourages the truth in your identity and sense of safety.

4. Look back over the several Bible verses that are used in this chapter. Pick out one of the verses that most serves as an affirming truth to your identity or sense of safety. Share this verse with a friend or group, identifying why the verse makes an encouraging difference to you.

DAY THREE

— ◆ ◆ ◆ —

The Plan of Peace

It must have been a confusing and tough time for all who were connected to Jesus. The hours leading up to and including the crucifixion and death of the Savior were surely devastating as they saw all their hopes, dreams, and relationships come crashing down like a building that was imploded. But the day after the death and burial—that must have been depressing and painful to the point of being heart stopping.

We remember well the evening of and the day after the 9/11 attacks in 2001. *What is next?* we thought. *What will we do? How will we respond? Why is our nation hated so much?* Will we ever be safe again? These had to be some of the same questions that those early followers of Jesus were asking on Friday evening and Saturday after the crucifixion.

Then the most remarkable thing of all happened on Sunday morning. It started with a totally unexpected encounter between Jesus and Mary.

Mary, her heart crushed with grief, went to the tomb with no hope and no hope of finding hope. Grief does this to people. They stumble around from place to place, searching for something to reassemble a direction for their lives. Then the two angels and Jesus appeared to Mary and she remembered the conversations concerning the third day. Given instruction from Jesus to find the other disciples, she ran with a heart renewed with hope.

Every ounce of her being must have been poured into one question as she ran: *Was what I experienced real?* But she faithfully reported what she had seen

73

and heard. How the disciples must have been stunned—afraid to hope and afraid to face the resurrected Jesus if the hope was realized!

It is no surprise to us that, as a result of the morning report from Mary, the disciples were behind a locked door in the evening. Perhaps it was only because they were afraid of being caught and crucified themselves by the religious leaders, but they may also have had a little fear of this Jesus "ghost." But suddenly He was there with them, just like He had been with Mary in the morning. "Jesus came and stood among them and said to them, 'Peace be with you.' When he had said this, he showed them his hands and his side" (*John 20:19-20*).

In our culture, *peace* most often refers to a cessation of strife or war. In Jesus's culture, however, *shalom* would also carry the meaning of emotional calmness or fulfillment. All would be settled because all need, despair, or pain would be totally resolved.

In saying "Peace," perhaps Jesus was just giving a traditional greeting. But considering the context of the turmoil and strife the disciples were facing, Jesus was likely saying, "The battle has been won. Be at rest, knowing that I am here and all is now fulfilled."

Notice that Jesus still carried the wounds in His hands and side. In fact, it was these wounds that made Jesus recognizable and a reality to the disciples. The evidence of His suffering did not disappear like it had never happened. Instead, He continued to carry His death and passion with Him…with one conspicuous change: His injuries and death were not painful to Him anymore. Instead, the wounds were simply validation that Jesus had overcome all that was threatening and had resolved all that was wrong.

It had to be a remarkable time as the disciples began to experience, even with all their questions, the feeling that things were going to be okay.

The Plan

There are two tough realities that we must face as followers of Jesus coming into Day 3 of the work.

74

First, the Father, Jesus, and the Holy Spirit have accomplished some things that we could never have accomplished on our own. As in Jesus's resurrection, we have no hope of ever bringing about the process needed to make what is dead alive. Yet this is exactly what God has done for us, even though we could not accomplish it ourselves. As Paul put it, "Since we have been justified by faith, we have peace with God through our Lord Jesus Christ" (*Romans 5:1*). This is real if we are believers in and followers of Christ. God has freely given us grace, counted Christ's death as ours, and reconciled us to a peace where we can reestablish relationship for eternity. Our position is secure, and living into this reality of a new life under grace makes all the difference.

Except that the difference does not make the reality total.

The second tough reality we must deal with is that God clearly expects us to live into the new life. When Jesus ascended to heaven, the disciples were left to work out the process of putting the new into practice in the same world with limitations that looked very similar indeed. Likewise, God is at work among us and in us, yet He expects us to also be at work in making the new a reality in the midst of an old world. Paul described this process memorably when he said, "Work out your own salvation with fear and trembling" (*Philippians 2:12*).

It has never been the plan that the new self would mean the obliteration of the old self in this life. Like Jesus carrying the wounds in His hands and side even in His new resurrected body, you carry the old wounds to your identity and sense of safety as well as the Pain Cycle of reactivity and emotional disregulation. In the last chapter, you did much work to start the process of claiming the truth about your identity and safety and making it your own, but you likely realize that you still carry those doubts in the Pain Cycle that linger on even though you are sincere and want to be different.

Fortunately, the apostle Paul provides us with a secure and stable plan that at once acknowledges we have this new self God has brought into operation and yet gives clear direction on how we are to work alongside the Holy Spirit to make it more and more a reality in our everyday lives. Let us give you a longer version of a quote we cited earlier: "That is not the way you learned Christ!—assuming that you have heard about him and were taught in him, as the truth is in Jesus, to put off your old self, which belongs to your former manner of life and is corrupt through deceitful desires, and to be renewed in the spirit of your minds, and to put on the new self, created after the likeness of God in true righteousness and holiness" (*Ephesians 4:20-24*).

This is the plan God has laid out before us. We are to be fully aware of the old self and all the deceitful ways that have corrupted our identity, sense of safety, and behaviors. You have done this work in reckoning with yourself in Day 1. Then, through the "renewing of the spirit of our mind," we are to start the process of putting on the new self. You have started this work in Day 2 by coming to grips with the truth about your identity and sense of safety. We still have further to go to understand exactly what this new self looks like, but today's goal is not only to firmly set the truth about what you believe concerning identity and safety but also to formulate the new behavior that can result.

The Cognitive Map

It is important to remember that there are aspects of you, even in your current form, that are quite remarkable. Even if you came from circumstances that taught you the lies you were unloved and there was nothing you could do to survive in an unsafe world or relationship, these were not the only messages you received about identity and safety. You survived because someone loved you and provided you with safety.

One of our beefs with modern psychology is that it often concentrates so much on the problems of life that it neglects the truth that people are psychologically resilient. We will never forget Maya Angelou speaking one time about her tragic background and legacy of abuse. She spoke about how African Americans had lived through the gut-wrenching realities of slavery and all of the assaults that a people endured to their identity and sense of safety. She said, "The thinker must think! How have we survived?" Indeed, how did she and her people survive?

In the same speech, she spoke about the faith many of her race had to move forward and sang the hymn "I Shall Not Be Moved." She also talked about a family member who faithfully sat with her many evenings each week reviewing the multiplication tables with her because he believed that education would be a strengthening and healing factor in her life. In the midst of so many things that were out of control, here were people who were exercising the elements of love and trustworthiness in small ways that strengthened her ability to know who she was and believe she could do something different in a world that was unpredictable and unjust.[5]

It was how Maya Angelou survived. It is how African Americans survived. Indeed, it is how all who have suffered tragic and repeated insults to safety and identity have survived.

When we stabilize ourselves with the truth of love and trustworthiness, we start moving toward the sense of peace that Christ was speaking about after His resurrection. Whether we feel this love and trustworthiness from family, from friends, from God, or—most powerfully—from ourselves, it stabilizes our identity and sense of safety and starts to open new possibilities in our behaviors. Instead of the pain that results from disregulated primary emotions, we have the possibility of experiencing shalom. We can feel a sense of rest, fulfillment, and contentment because our needs have been met and our pain has been answered. As a result of knowing who we are and that we are safe, we feel peace.

As the illustration below indicates, this gives us a new opportunity, not based on the reactivity of fight or flight when our brain feels stress, but by relieving us of the need for automatic reactions and opening the possibility of choosing our behaviors rationally and intentionally. When we make these rational and intentional choices, we are not bound in the reactive part of our midbrains but instead are operating in the calm part of our prefrontal cortex.

When we are at peace, we have the ability to choose to do good by others and ourselves. We call this choice of behavior *agency.*

Expression of Love (Identity) and Trustworthiness (Safety)

Results In...

Primary Emotions of Feeling Loved and Safe

Leads to Agency of...

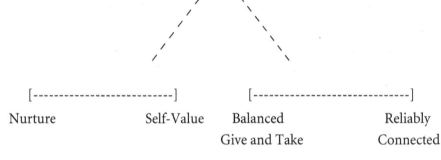

[-------------------------]		[----------------------------]
Nurture	Self-Value	Balanced	Reliably
		Give and Take	Connected

Notice how the above illustration contrasts with the illustration on page 32 in Day 1. Blame, shame, control, and escape behaviors do not happen because you are a bad person. These behaviors occur in a semi-automatic fashion because they are fight/flight reactions to emotionally being out of whack with your sense of identity and safety. In other words, when you feel unsafe or unloved, you do not think about being destructive as much as you simply react destructively. But contrast that reality with the illustration above. When you feel loved and safe, you feel a sense of contentment, fulfillment, and peace. There is no stress, pressure, or urge to do something destructive, because there is no reactivity.

Here, you are exposed to the truth about the identity that you are perfectly loved and know you are special and worthy and you belong. Also, you are in the truth concerning your sense of safety. You are safe because you are empowered to do things to protect yourself and, when situations are emotionally painful, you know that they often yield necessary growth and ultimately "good." You are also safe because you are not alone.

Jesus said, "You will know the truth and the truth will set you free" (John 8:32). Knowing this truth leads you to be able to make a choice about how you behave. You now have the freedom to nurture, self-value, live in balanced give-and-take, and reliably connect.

Nurture.

When you are in a reactive state, you have a tendency to blame others, which can result in being aggressive, retaliatory, angry, sarcastic, and punishing. Words can indeed be harmful, as we are reminded by James: "The tongue is a fire, a world of unrighteousness. The tongue is set among our members, staining the whole body, setting on fire the entire course of life, and set on fire by hell" (*James 3:6*). Most of us, at one time or another, have let blaming and toxic words come out of our mouths. Many times, it is like we are in slow motion watching those words come from our lips when we know they will do damage to the hearer.

Nurture stands as the perfect opposite to this kind of blaming reactivity. There are many things we can do in nurturing others, but practically, we put our focus on three behaviors.

First, we can *listen*. It is a rare and magical thing we give to people when we allow them to be heard. It communicates respect and trustworthiness to individuals we care about simply by making sure they know we consider them worthy of uninterrupted focus and they are the priority in the process. It also nurtures the individual by helping this person understand himself or herself better.

Many times we come home and are emotionally upset or frustrated about something at work. In our relationship, when the other takes the time to listen in a respectful way without answering questions, pointing out mistakes, or giving alternatives, both of us usually find that our processing allows us the time and space to clarify the sequence of events, and our thoughts about them, and allows us to see where our emotions come into play.

How many times have you sat with a friend and simply let him or her complain, express, or cry, and at the end of the time, the friend expressed to you that he or she felt better simply because of being heard? In reality, when we listen, we give others the opportunity to also listen to themselves and organize their thoughts. When we listen, people feel respected, cared about, and understood.

There are some good rules to follow when you listen. You should not give advice or interject your own stories too much. Also, you can be helpful if you summarize what you have heard from the other person from time to time, especially using words and phrases that the individual has used. You must also be attentive. To nurture by listening, you have to look at the other person's face and not be distracted by electronics or other conversations. If you listen in this way, you will also give an individual nurture because he or she will feel you empathize. This empathizing is a key component in making an individual feel like he or she is not alone.

A seven-year-old girl was walking home from school and was a bit late. Her mother asked, "Where were you and why were you late?"

"Oh, Mother," she said, "I was on my way home and I saw Sarai sitting on the curb crying. When I asked her what was wrong, she told me that some mean boys ran up, took her doll out of her hands, and broke the head of her doll off."

Her mother said with a glare, "So you stopped to help Sarai fix her doll?"

The little girl answered, "No, Mother. I stopped to help Sarai cry."

When you listen, at times you most likely will not be able to fix anything with the circumstance or the feeling of another individual. The point is, however, that the individual will feel better because he or she is nurtured.

The second practical thing you can do when nurturing others is to *encourage*. There are many ways to encourage someone, but we most often think of encouragement as calling out to the individual what is true about his or her identity and how he or she acts in the world. There is almost nothing that is more encouraging to us than when someone affirms the very thing that we most desire to do.

From time to time, we hear something like the following: "I remember you speaking about the Pain Cycle a few years ago at a community group. There have only been a few times in my life when I heard something and thought, *This is important and will change my life.* I want you to know that I paid attention and it has changed my life."

These kinds of encouraging statements can keep us going and keep us building into others' lives.

The same is true when we call out such things about a person's identity. Terry often says to Sharon, "Everything good in my life is connected to you." Sharon often says to Terry, "You are the best thing that has happened to me." We call out each other's gifts and talents, such as intelligence, creativity, generosity, wisdom, and care. We call out traits such as thoughtfulness, loyalty, hard work, and dedication. We name and reinforce the truth to one another, saying, "You are loved. You are special. God is at work through you. You are not alone. You are more than enough. You are safe in God's economy."

When you take the time to call these truths out loud to another, you are actually speaking straight to the heart and initiating a blessing. It is an affirmation of the belief about the truth and becomes a powerful motivator of healthy identity and safety.

A third thing you can do in the process of nurturing others is accept another person. Acceptance is a gift of nurture because it communicates to the receiver that, no matter what he or she has done or left undone, you understand and will not leave. Acceptance is a type of loyalty and love that communicates, "I will never be ashamed of you, and you will always maintain a preferred status in my heart."

It is important to note here that acceptance does not mean approval, simply because all of us do things that are regrettable and are not okay. Think about the story of the prodigal son. He had committed a great wrong toward his father and brother and had promoted evil in his life. Yet his father willingly accepted him back, assuring him that he was loved and would always maintain the position of son. The father did not excuse his wrongdoing, but his position of being favored and loved remained unthreatened (*Luke 15:11-24*).

When we nurture using acceptance, we communicate compassion, patience, and unwavering love.

Self-value.

In *Winnie the Pooh*, Eeyore always manages to see the gloomy side of things and is consistently negative and depressed. We all have a little "Eeyore" in us at times when we are feeling unloved and as if we cannot measure up. The real difference in people who are emotionally disregulated with their identity and sense of safety and react by shaming themselves is that their "Eeyore" is the only person who shows up in behavior. In short, they simply refuse to see any possibilities other than the situation is hopeless to feel loved or safe and they are powerless to affect life.

Shame is particularly toxic to the personhood of an individual because it affirms the most negative and harmful aspects of identity. For instance, when Terry shames himself for not being as smart as other professors or colleagues, he pronounces himself as being inadequate. When he longs for affirmation from someone, he reinforces that he is unloved every time someone fails to recognize him in the way he wants them to express care and love. All of our reactivity tends to violate love and trustworthiness, but shame is so difficult because the shaming directly assails our sense of love and identity. If, however, we can start with the perspective of truth about our identity and sense of safety, then we start to create the possibility of meaningfully valuing ourselves and taking responsibility to manage our environment positively.

There are several practical ways a person can engage in this self-value.

It is helpful for shamers to treat themselves as people worthy of respect. Few of us would ever speak openly to others about how they are unloved, unwanted, or incapable. Yet, as shamers, we are mostly unabashed in giving ourselves this message both verbally and silently in our heads many times a day. To treat ourselves with respect first of all means that we will say nothing about ourselves (silently or verbally) that we would not be willing to say out loud about another.

Another self-valuing exercise we can do is to stop selectively filtering messages. Most of us who shame tend to give ear to only the messages that currently fit with our self-image. We tend to filter out any feedback or information that shows us in a positive light and to focus almost exclusively on the shaming message.

We see this often with people who suffer with body image problems. When these folks look at themselves in the mirror, they usually see nothing they like, even though there is much there to celebrate. Instead of seeing great hair, a beautiful smile, or good tone, they will say things like "I am carrying too much weight" or "I hate the way my nose looks" or "My eyes are so small."

Of course, it is not just people with body image problems that have this tendency to selectively filter information. When I (Terry) was moving several years ago, I was cleaning out some old professional correspondence. I came across a review of the first article I wrote for publication. The review was brutal and negative in many ways and certainly contributed to my own shame when I had received it years before. When I read it over, it brought back all the same doubts and same shaming attitudes I had when I first received it. It made me wonder why I had kept such a toxic letter, and I determined to find the letters in the file that were positive reviews and resulted in publications.

Interestingly, I could not find one of these letters. I had kept the letter that made me feel the worst about myself but had discarded all the letters that would affirm the gifts and talents I possess.

This selective filtering of negative messages is the antithesis of self-valuing and is what shamers excel in doing to themselves. Stopping this selective filtering and taking in the affirming and positive messages we receive about our actions and personhoods are essential in the valuing of self.

Finally, it is important in the agency of self-valuing to give positive and affirming messages to ourselves.

We often think of the Golden Rule that we should love others in the way we wish to be loved. Our take on this type of love is slightly different than you might have heard before. Jesus said, "A new commandment I give to you, that you love one another: just as I have loved you, you also are to love one another" (*John 13:34*). Instead of thinking that we should love ourselves so we can love others, Jesus clearly states in this verse that He wants us to love just as He has loved us. By extension, it makes sense that we not only need to love one another like Jesus loves us but also we need to love *ourselves* as Jesus loves us.

In short, we are talking about self-value through nurturing ourselves: To lovingly nurture ourselves with encouragement in calling out our own gifts, virtues, and characteristics. To make sacrifices for ourselves to make sure we get the food, sleep, and exercise we need to be our best. To give ourselves time and space to connect with what is life-giving instead of life-detracting.

This does not mean we are perfect or blind to our faults and limitations. Self-valuing does not mean we become self-aggrandizing or narcissistic. We can honestly look at ourselves and deal with correction without shaming ourselves into self-mutilating behaviors.

Shaming ourselves not only does us harm, but it also negates the message of love that we seek to give to others. As Maya Angelou once said, "I don't trust people who don't love themselves and tell me, 'I love you.'... There is an African saying which is: Be careful when a naked person offers you a shirt." [6]

Balanced give-and-take.

At first glance, it may not be clear why a balance of give-and-take is an answer to controlling reactive behavior. The answer is found in the degree of vulnerability that the balance of give-and-take requires.

When we control out of our pain, we basically are making a statement of self-dependence and self-reliance affirming that we will not risk putting our lives or our fates in the hands of some other person's actions or reputation. As we said in the Day 1 chapter, relationships and trust demand a sense of justice or balance between give and take. At the heart of a controller is a drive that says, "I will trust no one, and I am better off fending for myself. In those places where I must depend on someone else, I must be vigilant to make sure he or she does things the way I approve and would do them myself." Thus the controller seldom engages in true vulnerability or anything that vaguely resembles a dependence on another person.

Balanced give-and-take, on the other hand, demands that the controlling person realize that he or she cannot do everything nor that he or she has the best ideas about the way everything needs to be done.

We are built to be interdependent. The New Testament makes this point about the church: "As in one body we have many members, and the members do not all have the same function, so we, though many, are one body in Christ, and individually members one of another" (*Romans 12:4-5*). We may think we are an island apart from the rest of humanity and we call our own shots about life, but here Scripture tells us that we are just one part of the whole and we cannot function without the rest. We are interdependent in the way God crafted us from the beginning in that people need the gifts, talents, and personhood we bring to the table, just as we need the same from them.

To be balanced in give-and-take is to first recognize we are dependent upon others for healthy functioning. Simply stated, we cannot do what others can *only* do for us. As we actively acknowledge that we cannot do everything ourselves, we start seeing the things others contribute that are of value and for which we can depend upon them.

I (Sharon) was a coordinator of a vacation Bible school when my children were younger. In my opinion, it was the best run, most successful, and most or-ganized vacation Bible school in the history of our church. We had the highest attendance; we had the most volunteers; and the programs yielded great benefit to our families. I was so pleased.

But in the midst of it, I learned something about myself.

On the second to last day, I was going my rounds to make sure that everyone was doing their job just as I had it planned. On my way down a hall, my co-coordinator jokingly said to me, "Hey, Sharon, stop acting like a pit bulldog with PMS!"

We laughed together, but I knew there was an edge to the comment.

Shortly after this, I noticed when I went into the break room that the other teachers immediately snapped to and said things like "What do we need to be doing?"

It seems that everywhere I went the atmosphere switched from being relaxed and effective to being tense and solution focused.

Later that day I was speaking to a woman who was charged with gathering the supplies for the arts and crafts. Honestly, I cannot imagine a worse job, and it is one that would make me totally frustrated and overwhelmed. But this woman affirmed, "I have loved this process so much. It fits my nature and creativity to think about how things can be reused, and I love contacting folks to contribute. I don't feel like I am cut out for teaching, but I really feel at home in making sure supplies are there for those who can teach. It is my gift!"

I cannot do what this woman did so easily. If I would have tried to get her to do it my way, we both would have ended up frustrated. The truth was, I needed this woman to do what she did so all of us could work together to make a wonderful vacation Bible school.

But here is the deeper truth: even in the areas where I thought I had competence and ideas, such as teaching and organization, I equally needed those others who were making their contributions. It is true that I had something to give and an important part to play, but it was only a part and it was important for me to learn how to accept from others what only they could give to the effort. When I paused and started to accept that I was only part of the working mission, I suddenly became more relaxed, less rigid in my thinking, and more open to others' ideas and actions.

Accepting our need for others is part of the story in becoming balanced in the give-and-take of relationship. But learning to be flexible is just as essential.

As controllers, we often think in terms of perfection and protection, as in "If I do things perfectly, then I cannot be criticized and I will always be safe." We are not making a case to do less than our best, but humans simply are not built for perfection. We chronically make mistakes and are prone to fallibility. We cannot predict the future and therefore cannot predict all the correct actions to ultimately protect ourselves. For instance, we can manage our finances wisely and frugally, but our actions do not guard against a downturn in the economy, job loss, or an investment that goes wrong. When we are at peace emotionally, we have the opportunity to employ more flexibility in our thinking and realize that perfection and absolute protection are impossible to achieve. As we give up this fantasy of ultimate control, we find ourselves in the place where we can hear others' ideas and employ them—or let them employ them—without judgment or protest.

Flexibility encourages our willingness to accept others' ideas and actions in such a way that we acknowledge our need for others. The human body provides the analogy. "The eye cannot say to the hand, 'I have no need of you,' nor again the head to the feet, 'I have no need of you' " (*1 Corinthians 12:21*). This kind of flexibility begins the give-and-take between us and others and serves us to be able to build trust and deeper reliance on relationships. This reliance then starts the process of increasing our vulnerability to others and we begin to see real progress in letting go and stopping our controlling behaviors.

One more practical thing we can do to start building a balance in our give-and-take: intentionally do what others suggest from time to time. As you start this self-discipline, it might look like shopping at a place that is your less than favorite store, taking a route with which you are totally unfamiliar, or going to a movie or concert you would normally reject. But as you start doing these small things that do not matter greatly, you will likely notice that many of the things were really not bad ideas at all. More importantly, you will likely notice that the quality of your relationships begins to improve substantially.

These small efforts to cooperate with the natural flow of give-and-take in relationships will likely lead you to take more risks, such as spending time or money on efforts that are unfamiliar to you or out of your control or doing projects the way another believes they should be done. There are seldom flashes of insight that substitute for actually practicing taking in what others think and then doing it the way they think or suggest. The practice makes us employ the discipline of dependence and flexibility.

Reliably connecting.

Let us be real and honest: life is difficult. As we have discussed before, life is full of difficult situations, relationships, and people as well as physical threats. Many times, we feel the necessity of wanting to escape these difficulties and give ourselves space and time to see if the problems will subside or at least to take a respite from the challenge. This seems reasonable, does it not? This is the heart of one of the more perplexing difficulties with withdrawal, escape, and irresponsibility: it seems as if we are not hurting anyone or anything by checking out of life for a while.

"What harm does it cause anyone if I drink to take the edge off a difficult situation?"

"Whose business is it if I play video games for hour upon hour, if I eventually get my work done?"

"What is the problem with just walking away from difficult people or situations, because the stress will always be there when I return?"

Some of us even take the position that it is better if we withdraw or escape.

"So I leave the conversation and go hang out at the bar and watch the game. If I were to stay, I would end up getting angry and doing far worse damage."

"I can't see how being stressed by relationships and injuring my health is any worse than going to work and staying there for fourteen hours."

Maybe these things seem reasonable to you also.

The problem with escape is threefold.

First, the escape or withdrawal tends to become habitual and can even become addictive. It is easy to see how drinking alcohol regularly can modify our brains and body to the point where we become physiologically addicted and need the substance to function. But we also know that certain repeated behaviors, such as over-involvement with technology, gambling, or pornography, can also modify us to a point where we become psychologically dependent on the activity the same as if we were addicted. Once addicted or habituated, however, we choose to perform the activity or use the substance every time we are triggered by our Pain Cycle.

This leads us to the second issue with escape or withdraw. It begins to promote unreliable behavior. We do not show up for the people who are depending upon us to do our part in relationships. We know that, in order to build trustworthiness in relationships, it takes predictable and stable behavior about eight or nine times out of every ten. Simply stated, if we do not show up, or if we show up intermittently, we destroy our reputation for trustworthiness.

Finally, when we escape, we tend to become passive participants in life. Instead of taking responsibility for our own choices, we withdraw and force others either to count on other people instead of us or to facilitate our irresponsible behavior by being over-controlling. Either way, passivity takes away an individual's power to chose his or her course of action in life and relationships and usually results in irresponsible behaviors that breed chaos.

Let us reemphasize, however, that life is difficult. How, then, do we step into this difficult reality and stay present and reliably connect instead of escaping?

First, there is a peace that comes from knowing that staying connected with others will eventually help us work toward a resolution of the problems we face. Withdrawal or escape leaves problems, but it tends to leave them alive and kicking whenever we return. Staying reliably connected means we stay the course with a difficult situation until the situation resolves in some way.

Sharon's mother, Genevieve, had wise words about this. Remember that this is a woman who faced the suicide of her husband, the death of her oldest son due to illness, and the murder of her next oldest son. During tough times, she repeated, "If we hold each other close, things will be okay." These words keep ringing in our ears as a testimony to stay reliably connected.

It is not that Genevieve was saying we will immediately feel different after tragedy. Rather, she meant that if we just kept on holding on to connection with one another, we will eventually find a way to make it through difficulty.

Her dedication to staying connected reminds us that God is in charge of difficult times and that, if we stay present in the problem and our relationships, we will see it through to the other side and find rest and peace. The Bible offers the same encouragement to stick with it: "No temptation has overtaken you that is not common to man. God is faithful, and he will not let you be tempted beyond your ability, but with the temptation he will also provide the way of escape, that you may be able to endure it" (*1 Corinthians 10:13*).

Second, there is a discipline of peace that comes from remaining reliably connected instead of withdrawing or escaping. The reality is that, when we escape or withdraw, we never learn anything new, nor do we build any sense of virtue or character. Only by engaging life do we learn, grow, and mature. As one biblical proverb says, "Whoever ignores instruction despises himself, but he who listens to reproof gains intelligence" (*Proverbs 15:32*).

As we have stated before, pain tends to bring about growth and maturity that we could never achieve without it. It does not matter whether this pain comes from death and loss, tragedy, stress and difficulties at work, hard-to-live-with people, or problem family or other close relationships. If we stay connected to the relationship or situation, pain will teach us.

Now it is time to identify those behaviors you want to make sure fit into your new-self cognitive map. You should think of the behaviors you identify in the next exercise as the automatic winners you can use to consistently build loving and trustworthy actions toward yourself and others in relationships. Many times, these words you choose will be the opposites of what you identified in your Pain Cycle. You should, however, focus on the behaviors that flow out of you naturally when you are in touch with your truth that produces a sense of peace concerning your identity and safety.

EXERCISE 10
Choosing What You Will Do

1. Look back at the truths you identified in Exercise 8, page 59. Concentrate on these words and let the reality of these truths about your identity and safety soak in. Write down these words below so you can remember them easily.

2. Now look at the list of words below that describe different actions. When you are focused on the truth you identified, what are the actions you would chose to do or would likely naturally take instead of the coping behaviors listed in your Pain Cycle? Circle two to five actions that best describe what you would choose to do when you are in your truth and feel a sense of peace.

Loving	Values Self	Balanced Give/Take	Responsible
Encouraging	Respects Self	Vulnerable	Reliable
Supportive	Positive	Open	Self Controlled
Inclusive	Humble	Engaging	Connected
Kind	Optimistic	Appreciative	Intimate
Listening	Hopeful	Imperfect	Faithful
Accepting	Self-Aware	Relaxed	Forthcoming
Patient	Confident	Lets Things Go	Problem Solving
Compassionate	Other Focused	Spontaneous	Planning

3. Take a few moments and consider the words you have circled above. Are there any actions you would say flow from you naturally when you are at your best or feel peaceful that are not listed above? If so, write these additional words below.

_____

_____

Putting Your New-Self Cognitive Map Together

You have not been dominated by disregulating emotions in your identity and sense of safety. There have been times you have felt peaceful. It is important to remember that the Holy Spirit has already prepared you with remarkable abilities, giftedness, and talents to join the mission of God. But it is likely that you have never organized yourself to understand this new-self map. Listing these truths and actions together can be a powerful tool in shaping your mind. Just like a construction plan gives an accurate picture of the final product, so this new-self map can help you know what your best self looks like.

For instance, Sharon's Peace Cycle is listed below. The phrase "Safe in God's economy" is a modification of the word "Safe" that helps Sharon personalize her fears about the world being out of control, so that she knows that, no matter what happens, good will be produced in the end. She also has an identity piece of "Not alone" that regulates the emotion of feeling alone. When she gets in touch with these truths, it stabilizes her disregulated feelings of being unsafe and alone. You can easily contrast this with Sharon's Pain Cycle.

When she stabilizes the feelings with the truth, she feels a sense of peace and is able to choose balanced give-and-take and nurturing. Again, you can easily contrast these with her Pain Cycle reactive coping of controlling behavior and blame and anger.

Sharon's Pain Cycle

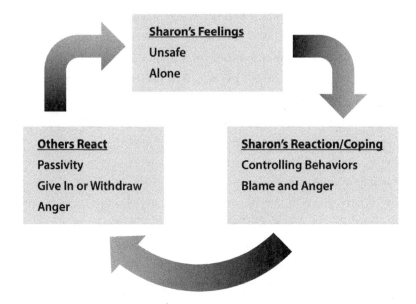

Sharon's Feelings
Unsafe
Alone

Sharon's Reaction/Coping
Controlling Behaviors
Blame and Anger

Others React
Passivity
Give In or Withdraw
Anger

Sharon's Peace Cycle

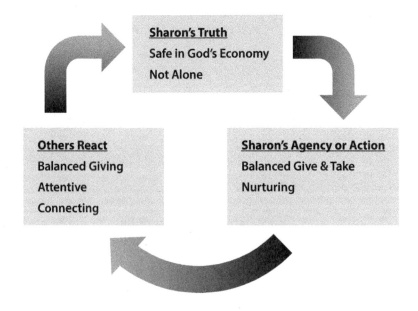

Sharon's Truth
Safe in God's Economy
Not Alone

Sharon's Agency or Action
Balanced Give & Take
Nurturing

Others React
Balanced Giving
Attentive
Connecting

You can see how the cycle works. In the Pain Cycle, others react to Sharon's controlling behaviors and anger with passivity, withdrawal, and anger. This, in turn, makes it more likely that Sharon will feel more disregulation in her sense of safety and identity. She will feel more unsafe and more alone.

But when we contrast that with her Peace Cycle, we see that others react to her balanced give-and-take and nurturing by participating in their part of giving and taking, being attentive, and connecting with her. These actions by others re-inforce her regulating truths that she is safe in God's economy (things will work out in the end) and that she is not alone.

The Peace Cycle produces a spiraling upwards of truth and agency that creates more and more emotional regulation and opportunity for Sharon's best self to come out. The Pain Cycle creates the same type of spiral, but the direction will always be downward as she feels worse about her identity and safety and others are injured more and more by her reactive coping.

We all prefer to be around people who are emotionally regulated and stable in their Peace Cycle. But the deeper truth is that, when we operate out of this new-self Peace Cycle behavior, we like ourselves better. We find ourselves operating in cooperation with the Holy Spirit instead of being at war with where God wants us to go. We find ourselves integrating and living out a deeper level of discipleship as well as a deeper level of personhood as we build love and trust-worthiness in our relationships.

Now it is your turn to put down the blueprint of your new self in the following exercise. This is your Peace Cycle, and it will become the essential element of replacing and regulating your Pain Cycle.

EXERCISE 11
Creating Your Peace Cycle

Look back at the truths you identified in Exercise 8 , page 59, and write down these words in the box marked "Truths."

Now look back at the actions you identified in the last Exercise 10, page 92, and write down these words in the box marked "Actions."

Finally, think about how others behave or react to you consistently when you do what you do in your actions. Write these reactions down in the box marked "Others React."

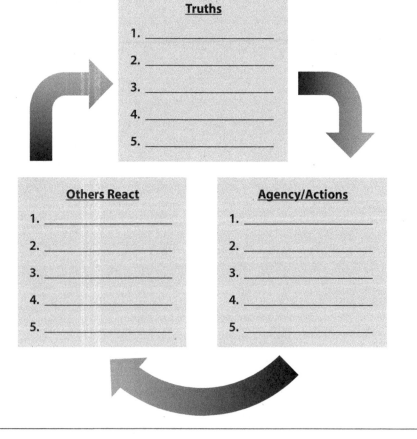

Truths

1. _____
2. _____
3. _____
4. _____
5. _____

Others React

1. _____
2. _____
3. _____
4. _____
5. _____

Agency/Actions

1. _____
2. _____
3. _____
4. _____
5. _____

A Day of Exploring New Territory

Imagine yourself a little over two centuries ago in the Corps of Discovery along with Meriwether Lewis and William Clark as they blazed a trail from the Mississippi River to the Pacific Ocean. Every step they took was new territory to them, and so they organized their experience through making a map and then risked plenty to keep that map and their records safe.

On this third day, you have done much work to explore new territory in your life. Perhaps you recognized some of it before, but chances are, you have never taken the time to organize it into a map you can use to make sense of your emotional being. This is the day when you mapped your new self, and we can tell you it makes it much more likely that you will be able to find yourself in the future and get to the place where you want to be, not only in your relationship with God, but also in your relationships with yourself and others.

Day 3 is about defining your place and your actions that are formed by peace. This peace is a place that produces a new freedom where you can choose behaviors that will work and be loving and trustworthy.

God is rooting for you in this new freedom because it perfectly fits within the vision the Spirit has for you. Your Peace Cycle is more than just a way to get along in life; it actually is a map and picture of how to become what you are in Christ—a person who is molded to and becoming more and more like Jesus. The apostle Paul says, "Now the Lord is the Spirit, and where the Spirit of the Lord is, there is freedom. And we all, with unveiled face, beholding the glory of the Lord, are being transformed into the same image from one degree of glory to another. For this comes from the Lord who is the Spirit" (*2 Corinthians 3:17-18*).

You have much to practice in becoming a new self, but you have viewed the ocean in your own Corps of Discovery.

For Reflection

1. God makes us new creations and expects us to work on the process of becoming the new self. What are the ways you have worked in concert with God to develop your best or new self? In what ways have you resisted working on this new self and promoted destructive or unproductive behavior? Discuss some of your thoughts with a friend or a group.

2. Think about an incident in your life when you operated from a place of peace where you felt right about yourself and felt good about relationships. What do you notice about your behaviors when you were operating in this good place? How are these behaviors from this incident like and unlike the behaviors you identified in the Peace Cycle? Share this story and your thoughts about your behaviors with a friend or a group.

3. Draw your Pain and Peace Cycles side by side on a single sheet of paper. As you look at the cycles, do they seem accurate to you? Is the contrast between the two clear to you? If you see problems in the cycles, what adjustments do you need to make in them so that they more accurately fit your life?

4. Talk with a friend or a group about your Peace Cycle. Be sure to refer to the elements of the truth you identified and the actions that result when you are in a place of peace. Now tell the friend or group how this Peace Cycle contrasts with your Pain Cycle. Ask your friend or the group if they see these contrasting elements (feelings, reactions/coping, truth, actions) in you and your behavior. Ask them to help you identify any part of your behaviors that they see that you did not identify.

5. Read again the last Bible quote in this chapter (*2 Corinthians 3:17-18*). Now take a look at your Peace Cycle. Do you feel that living in this Peace Cycle would help you in becoming more like the image or "glory" of Christ? Where would you like to be in your process of becoming a new self in one month? In one year? Share with a friend or group your thoughts, hopes, and new-self dreams.

DAY FOUR

◆ ◆ ◆

The Moment of Truth

We all have seen the moment of truth at a sporting event. The moment when a swimmer is tantalizingly close to a record at the end of a race. The agonizing time as the skaters with a chance for a medal wait anxiously for the judges' scores. The game when our team is ahead by one goal but the favored team is pressing hard at our end. The batter at the plate with a full count, two outs, bases loaded, and his team behind two runs. The moment of truth when the result will be determined one way or another: the record broken, the medal won, the win preserved, the hit made—or not. But success at the moment of truth (at least the part of the success that the individual or team can do something about) is heavily dependent upon this person's training, preparation, attention in the moment, and effort to perform.

We, too, are facing a moment of truth. Through the first three days of our work, we have seen that we have a clear choice between our Pain Cycle and our Peace Cycle. Will we do what it takes to actually start living out of our Peace Cycle?

The Pain Cycle goes into operation when negative emotions regarding our identity and sense of safety are triggered by some situation or relationship. When living out our Pain Cycle, we are likely to take destructive actions such as blame, shame, control, or escape because we have practiced those actions over and over again in our lives. The Pain Cycle is our "stuff," no matter the situation or what the other person is doing in the relationship.

But we have an alternative to just following our feelings and letting the same destructive cycle take place. We have a Peace Cycle and a new map for a new self. We have the ability to speak truth to ourselves that directly contradicts the emotional triggers. These truths are the fundamental beliefs about our identity and the sense of safety we want for ourselves, the same way a good parent wants stable love and trustworthiness for his or her child. There are many other important people and the living God who believe those truths about us and our situations. And finally we have a choice. If we let truth into us, it will produce a sense of peace, giving us the freedom to choose constructive behaviors that are nurturing, self-valuing, balanced in give-and-take, and reliable in connection.

We know what it is like to follow our feelings in the Pain Cycle and the destruction it will yield, and now we know we have a choice to follow the Peace Cycle. The situation or relationship represents our moment of truth. What direction will we follow?

In our day and culture, we have a bias toward the belief that you must do what your feelings tell you to do so that you are true to yourself. It is as if we are saying that our feelings are the most real things about us. But this is a great lie. Frankly, our feelings about our identity and sense of safety are wildly erratic and unpredictable. Following our feelings, and acting based on these lies, produces nothing that vaguely resembles peace.

It is only when we start with what we would responsibly tell ourselves about ourselves and about how the world works that we begin to settle into the truth leading to peace. Scripture teaches the same thing. For example, Peter said, "Preparing your minds for action and being sober-minded, set your hope fully on the grace that will be brought to you at the revelation of Jesus Christ. As obedient children, do not be conformed to the passions of your former ignorance, but as he who called you is holy, you also be holy in all your conduct" (*1 Peter 1:13-15*). The message of much of the gospel is our moment of truth: Will we follow our feelings into the Pain Cycle, or will we follow the truth into the Peace Cycle?

We hope you, like us, will clearly declare your wish to follow the way of the

Peace Cycle. But we know this is a process and it is not easy. This day is about learning how to bring the necessary elements to bear that will be the right preparation, make us alert to the important situations, and give our best efforts to make our moments of truth lean into the Peace Cycle. The process that we will be teaching you is called *mindfulness,* and it is intended to bring our maximum thought processes to the table so we can change.

The Scriptures and Mindfulness

The term *mindfulness* gets tossed around a lot and is often tied to Eastern thought. It is most often thought of as a way of becoming more aware of our thoughts, physical being, and emotions in a nonjudgmental and accepting manner. The way we are using the term, however, is a little different. To us, mindfulness is the awareness of what is going on in our thoughts, physical being, and emotions so we can free ourselves to make constructive choices about beliefs about ourselves and decisions regarding our actions in situations and relationships.

The apostle Paul was focused on this issue over two thousand years ago. Paul had a complicated past, being a Jewish leader and persecutor of the new religion of Christ. He felt he was doing right, but then he met Jesus and saw clearly how the old must pass away and how he was to become more and more like the Christ who saved him. In the first eleven chapters of the book of Romans, he laid out a theological case for how Christ accomplished this saving grace for us. In his presentation, we see over and over again how we were hopeless in our sin and how our hearts can be made new through the loving grace and sacrifice of Jesus. Paul emphasizes again and again the condition of our hearts, finally saying that if we confess and believe in our hearts the message of Christ, we can begin this new relationship.

In the first eleven chapters of Romans, Paul makes a clear case that the most essential element in making change happen in our lives is our hearts. Yet, after we believe in Christ and are charged with becoming like Him and joining His mission, the focus shifts away from the heart. In Romans 12:1-2, Paul says, "I appeal to you therefore, brothers, by the mercies of God, to present your bodies as a living sacrifice, holy and acceptable to God, which is your spiritual worship. Do not be conformed to this world, but be transformed by the renewal of your mind, that by testing you may discern what is the will of God, what is good and acceptable and perfect." It is a remarkable shift from talk about the change of heart to the reality that, if you are wanting to be different in the world, you must use your mind. If we look, however, we will find that this exhortation about the change to become like Christ through using the mind is actually a major theme in the New Testament.

Remember the "old self" and "new self" contrast from Ephesians? Here it is again: "That is not the way you learned Christ!—assuming that you have heard about him and were taught in him, as the truth is in Jesus, to put off your old self, which belongs to your former manner of life and is corrupt through deceitful desires, and to be renewed in the spirit of your minds, and to put on the new self, created after the likeness of God in true righteousness and holiness" (*Ephesians 4:21-24*). Did you catch it? *Be renewed in the spirit of your minds.* Again, we are called to change from the old Pain Cycle, which is much more reminiscent of our pre-Christ days, and use our minds to move toward the Peace Cycle of Christlikeness.

Paul puts forth the position again in Colossians, saying, "In these you too once walked, when you were living in them. But now you must put them all away: anger, wrath, malice, slander, and obscene talk from your mouth. Do not lie to one another, seeing that you have put off the old self with its practices and have put on the new self, which is being renewed in knowledge after the image of its creator" (*Colossians 3:7-10*). Here it is again, the idea that we put off the old and put on the new self by the *knowledge* we have in mind about the Creator. It begins to become clear that making a decision from the heart to accept the grace of Christ and be saved is not sufficient to produce cooperation with the Spirit to be transformed into His image. That takes a purpose of the mind, or *mindfulness*.

Paul wrote his letters long before neuroscience informed us about how to change our thinking. Yet most of what Paul said about change is consistent with what we know about how the brain brings about change.

What We Think We Know About the Brain

Recent years have produced a rapid increase in our understanding of the most remarkable part of the human system—the brain. Yet we have only begun to scratch the surface of how the brain functions.

Several facts about the brain defy our explanation.

To take one example, although we see patterns in how human brains process information, the sequences in how a brain functions differ from person to person. Most people (especially right-handed people) have the predominance of their language function on the left side of their brain. Yet there are a good number of people who have significant language function on the right side. Why? We don't know.

Here's another example. We humans are unique in our ability to think about our own thinking. In other words, we have the ability to be self-aware and analyze our own thoughts and behaviors as well as our patterns and feelings. It is likely part of the *imago dei* (image of God) that was breathed into us at creation. Science has no explanation for how this ability to think about ourselves happened or is learned.

These are just a couple of things that remind us that there is much more about the brain we do not know what we do know. But for our purposes, we can realize a few things will help us when we are trying to leverage our minds in order to produce more change.

All other things being equal, emotion is more powerful than cognition.

You would think that just knowing your Pain Cycle and Peace Cycle would be enough to produce change. After all, you likely think to yourself that it makes sense to follow this Peace Cycle more because you will be more satisfied with yourself and it is more consistent with your beliefs and faith. But chances are, you already realize that, even though the insight you gained thus far in this book is substantial, it is insufficient to produce change.

This has a physiological basis in the brain.

The midbrain is largely a nonthinking and nonreasoning part of your brain. It is where your systems are regulated and, most importantly, where threats are interpreted and acted upon in the fight-or-flight manner we mentioned before. From an extremely early age, your brain has been simply reacting to the messages of the midbrain. Particularly when the midbrain gets stimulated and reads some kind of threat in the environment, it mobilizes itself for action immediately. The cognitive part of your brain came on much later in your development and is used to cooperating with the motivations and reactions of the midbrain. Many times, our cognition simply does not question our midbrain reactions before we find ourselves taking action. You have likely heard the phrase "Think before you speak or act." This is a popular phrase because many times we find ourselves acting on our midbrain emotions before our prefrontal-cortex cognition is ready to take control.

Think of your emotions versus your cognition in this way: Emotions are like uncontrolled electricity. They are immense in power and are always trying to find a conductor to run through. They do not think about the damage they will do to the conductor nor even if the conductor can make use of the energy. Cognition, on the other hand, is like a wire connected to a toaster. If the wire is rightly connected to access the electricity, then the energy can be used in a fruitful and not destructive manner.

Cognition, by itself, is not as powerful as emotion, but it can utilize emotion in a productive manner. In order for cognition to make this work, it has to be made more powerful. In mindfulness terms, we make cognition more powerful by *attention* and *awareness.*

Your Pain Cycle is full of primary emotions and feelings about your identity and sense of safety. When these emotions are triggered, your tendency will be to let the cycle play out. You can make your cognition more powerful by practicing attention and awareness, particularly in situations where you are prone to get your buttons pushed.

We think of it like having a lookout at a watch post always being attentive and aware that the threat is present and ready to sound an alarm at any time the enemy presents. For instance, if you know your family pushes your buttons in your Pain Cycle, look for the warning signs of disregulated emotions going into the situation. If work challenges your sense of safety or identity, be on your guard when you walk in. Attention and awareness slow down the unbridled or natural reactions of the Pain Cycle emotions and give your cognition a chance to make a different choice.

Your brain is fast—really fast.

Think about how fast your computer or phone comes up with information. This is microprocessing at its finest and is a marvelous example of how far we have come in making machines work. But these items are not even close to the power of the brain. Current estimates tell us that the brain processes information at least nine thousand times as fast as the fastest microprocessor. It takes a mere thirteen milliseconds for the brain to process an image we see. This speed is astoundingly proficient and takes place with no special training or practice. But it is all the more impressive when combined with the amount of processing our brains handle every second. We have close to a billion neurons in our brains, and each one has about a thousand connections with other neurons and is capable of firing around two hundred messages per second. That makes us capable of processing around 20 million billion bits of information per second![7]

All of this speed, however, is not exactly our friend when it comes to getting a handle on our Pain Cycle. Speed means that we often are into our Pain Cycle, physiologically and emotionally, before we can get the leverage to slow down and consider an alternative. Think of it this way: your brain is going through a deck of cards, seeing every card, every few seconds. Left to itself, the brain will neither remember nor focus on the last card it saw, because it is already seeing and processing the current card. In order to get more leverage on changing old patterns in the brain, we have to slow down that processing to provide choice. In mindfulness, we have a fairly good idea that the way to slow down this processing is by *focusing* and *saying things out loud.*

Focusing on particular words or phrases tends to slow down processing, likely because it presents the same material in the brain over and over. Using the previous example, it keeps bringing up the same card again and again. You can focus by concentrating on particular words or phrases, but going back to images such as the Pain Cycle or writing your Pain Cycle out likely make the focus much more efficient and effective.

In addition, saying these words or phrases out loud moves the same information to different parts of the brain, allowing for more processing, more attention, and more leverage for the cognition. When I name something out loud, I must conceive of the word in my prefrontal cortex. I then must process this thought into a different section of my brain where sounds are assembled. From there, the thought must be connected to still another part of the brain where syntax and grammar are arranged. Finally, the process must be forwarded to my motor cortex, where the action of speaking is assembled and words come out of my mouth.

Furthermore, as I hear my own voice say the word or phrase, I once again increase my focus. All of this attention, focus, and saying the words or phrases out loud likely slows down my processing and allows my cognition to have more and more power in taking control over the Pain Cycle.

The brain prefers what it already knows.

Our brain, it turns out, is a creature of habit. For instance, although the average person has a vocabulary ranging from 15,000 to 20,000 words (meaning we know what these words mean and could use them if we chose to), most people actually use only around 750 to 1,000 different words per day. Even more astounding, 80 percent of the time, we use only about 120 to 150 words.[8]

We like what we already know, and it is difficult for us to adapt to new behaviors. If you have trouble believing this, try brushing your teeth tonight with the opposite hand from the one you normally use. You will likely find that it is cumbersome to do and problematic for your gums!

Our brains are efficient in learning and get used to particular neuronal sequences. It is like the neuronal connections in our brains are a snowcapped mountain. When the snow melts, the water finds its way down already existing ravines and gorges carved in the mountain. The connections already made are the ones that our brains are most likely to use.

This is not such good news if you want to stop the old-self Pain Cycle. These connections have been active in your brain for a long time and have been used in a sequential and predictable fashion thousands of times. When your primary emotions get triggered, your brain already has the neuronal connections well made and practiced to feel the emotions about your identity and safety and move to reactivity that is common in your Pain Cycle.

When working with people in our counseling practices, we often hear something like this: "In my saner moments, I swear to myself that I will not get angry and say something awful to my friend. But it seems like every time we are together, he says something that just slams me back to the same place. It can be his sarcasm, some strange political statement, or some action that makes no sense. Even though I have sworn that I am going to let those things pass, it is like I have a torch put to me and I am angry and I say the very things I swore I would not say. It seems so automatic, and I feel helpless when I can't seem to stop."

While the familiar responses are not truly automatic, this individual is feeling the pull of how the brain prefers what it already knows. The same thing happens to all of us.

How do we overcome this tendency?

While it is unfortunate that our brain is habituated to old behaviors such as the Pain Cycle, it does not take long for us to wear a new pathway in our neuronal network. For instance, it may be difficult for you the first time you brush your teeth with the opposite hand, but within ten times of practicing the behavior, you would find that you are becoming proficient at it.

Think of it like you are cutting a new trail in a jungle. The first trip requires much effort, planning, and probably many missteps. But the second trip through is much easier, as is each subsequent trip. Soon, if you keep using the trail, you will find the pathway well worn and easy to use compared to the first trip.

Such is the case with new behaviors in the brain. Left on its own, the brain will chose the pathway with which it is already familiar. But if challenged, the brain has a wonderful capability of learning new thoughts and behaviors and it adapts quickly. This ability to learn new things and change processing is called *neuroplasticity* and represents solid hope for us who long to change.

How does this apply to our Peace Cycle?

We give our new-self Peace Cycle a boost every time we are willing to *practice* the new truth and actions. Frankly, the first few times you practice your Peace Cycle it will feel quite clunky, like brushing your teeth with the opposite hand. But before long you will begin to see a difference.

For a good portion of my life, I (Terry) have worked on my anger. At the root of my anger is a feeling that I can never can make things turn out the way I want them to turn out or the way I feel entitled for them to turn out. When I fail or someone or something lets me down, I usually respond with anger in my Pain Cycle. So I have learned to keep telling myself the truth that, just because things did not work out the way I expected, the situation does not define me as a person and certainly does not mean failure.

One day, after dinner, we all were doing the dishes together as a family. It started out as a fun time, but more and more, our son and daughter were playing around and handling the dishes haphazardly.

I said, "All right, it is time to slow down before someone breaks one of the dishes."

Less than a minute had passed before my son, still in his playful mood, dropped a drinking glass. Not only did the glass shatter, but it also broke the floor tile beneath.

I still remember my family moving as if in slow motion, looking at the glass and the tile and then looking at me.

What felt natural was to say something like "I told you this would happen! Now look at what you have done!" But as my family looked at me, expecting the worst, I centered myself on the truth that this failure said nothing about me. I reminded myself that sometimes things just happen. I said, "It's okay. Mistakes happen."

My family looked at me as if to say, "That's it? That's all you are going to say? No anger?"

This was far from the last time I have gotten angry, but it might have been my first trip through the jungle cutting a new neural pathway in my brain and my first practice outside of my usual Pain Cycle. Certainly I am still practicing, but I can point to many times through wrecked cars, lost items, job disappointments, and just plain stupid mistakes that I have been able to practice my Peace Cycle successfully. Each time I am successful with the practice, the old-self Pain Cycle has less grip on me and the new-self Peace Cycle feels more familiar and easier.

All other things being equal, the brain will go negative.

This may be hard for the optimists among us to believe, but the truth is that the brain is heavily bent toward being negative. As psychologist Rick Hanson says, "The mind is like Velcro for negative experiences and Teflon for positive ones."[9] The brain is actually twice as likely to hold on to negative messages and interpret things negatively as it is to hold to positive thoughts or interpret things positively. This is not just the case for people who have the reactivity of shame; it is true for all of us.

There is a sound reason for why this happens. Our brain is built to look for potential threats, since we have significant survival drives and skills. Most of the things that are threatening to us are heavily processed in the part of the mid-brain that is emotionally charged. Any time you have a deeper emotional reaction combined with an experience, the experience will gather more of your focus, making it more likely that you will ruminate on the thought or experience and remember it longer.

Positive experiences are not processed in the part of the midbrain where these deeper emotional experiences are likely to happen. Without the emotional charge that comes with negative experiences, positive thoughts and experiences just do not stick and tend to not warrant focus or memory. Threat and anxiety are more often emotionally charged, while peace and fulfillment simply do not carry the emotional power.

There is a case that we are wired for negative thinking. Furthermore, there also is the reality that our brain likes to use the thoughts and processes it already knows well. In other words, once we become negative, we tend to be more and more negative in the future.

We have both struggled for years to take positive outlooks on life. For instance, when one of us would talk about a great vacation we had enjoyed as a family, the other would bring up the things that went wrong. When one of us would refer to an event that we were looking forward to, the other would often cast doubts about whether it would be good. While we were not negative all the time, we often hit the mark of being twice as negative as we were positive. Why? Of course both of us have had long experiences with negative threats and history that have impacted us deeply. Of course we are trained to be on the lookout for those things that can potentially go wrong and cause us additional pain. But the reality is that we tended to be more negative because we practiced negativity.

Hope is a fragile thing. While faith teaches us to trust that God is who He says He is and that He has done what He has said He has done (trust God's identity and actions), hope teaches us to believe God's promises and, in the absence of His promises, to trust in His character. God assures us that there is a plan for our good.

Joseph from the book of Genesis seems to have been a naturally positive guy, but his positive outlook and hopefulness resulted in a deep envy and hatred from his brothers. He was thrown down a hole, sold into slavery, wrongly accused of rape, and held in prison for years. Through miraculous dreams and prophecies, he was chosen to serve Egypt and prepare the region for a drought and famine. In all this, we have no sign that Joseph ever lost hope in God but rather see that he remained firm in the belief that God was at work with some kind of plan.

When his brothers came to Egypt because of the famine, he began to see how God was bringing to fruition the plan and how hope was being fulfilled. It culminated in one of the most remarkable positive statements of hope in the whole of the Scripture, when he said to his brothers, "You meant evil against me, but God meant it for good, to bring it about that many people should be kept alive, as they are today" (*Genesis 50:20*).

We must be honest with ourselves. Would we be as trusting and hopeful as Joseph at this point? Would we remain positive about how God was putting a plan into motion and we were serving as an essential part to save many? In our years of the practice of negativity, we have our doubts.

Our Pain Cycle has scientific and psychological roots, but it also has serious and substantial sinful roots that go into our very nature. If we are going to be able to change our old-self Pain Cycle to the new-self Peace Cycle, then we have to be intentional about being *positive* and *hopeful*. This begins with weeding out as many negative messages about our identity and sense of safety as possible and giving ourselves the positive and hopeful messages found in the truth.

You might think of this as positive "self-talk," but we like to think of it as hopeful "truth talk." We know that moving toward the positive and hopeful truth takes intentionality and time, but it does yield a sense of peace. Reminding ourselves again and again that God is at work and has not forgotten about us, even when it appears that nothing positive is happening, yields a sense of peace in time. Hope and positive thoughts are the antidote to the natural flow of negativity in the brain.

The brain does not think well under stress.

Study after study shows us that as stress, anxiety, and trauma increase in our experience, our ability to think clearly and make good decisions deteriorates. When we are in our Pain Cycle, we respond physiologically and our heart rates increase. Adrenaline and other stress chemicals pour into our system, preparing us for a fight or flight response. John Gottman, a relationship researcher, claims that it is almost impossible for us to have productive discussions and thinking when we our heart rate exceeds one hundred beats per minute and we are physiologically flooded.[10] Chances are, you would confirm his claims. When we reach that point of anger, fear, or stress, there are times when we simply must calm down in order to get the thinking part of our brains reengaged.

If we are going to get the leverage on our brains needed to change, we have to calm our bodies and our minds. There are a variety of ways that people achieve this that are simple to practice.

One option is deep breathing. You will be surprised what taking as little as thirty seconds breathing in and out slowly will do for your psychological flooding. Try and make these what we call "belly breaths," where you actually can feel your diaphragm move.

A second option is to work on a state of relaxation. There are various ways that people achieve this, but one tried and true way is to simply focus on an object while breathing deeply and imagine a more relaxing place, sound, or atmosphere.

Finally, points of meditation are always helpful. We recommend having a few Bible verses at the ready that bring you comfort and reassurance. Reading and contemplating these verses for even two minutes can make a tremendous difference in calming your physiology and psychology.

If left on your own, your body and brain will take twenty to thirty minutes to calm down after being emotionally disregulated. If you perform breathing, relaxation, or meditation, you likely will gain the effects of calming within five minutes.

Furthermore, paying attention to good physical health can add much to relieving stress. Eating well and regularly, sleeping eight to ten hours a day, maintaining a healthy exercise program, and engaging in varied activities you enjoy all contribute to your body's natural ability to combat stress and anxiety effectively. These are things you must practice consistently over a longer period of time than things like relaxation, breathing, and meditation, but they are just as important in building good brain habits where you have the ability to think and decide how to lean toward your Peace Cycle instead of your Pain Cycle.

EXERCISE 12
Practicing Emotional Regulation

1. Think about the things you just learned about the brain:
- Emotion is more powerful than cognition.
- Brain processing is fast.
- The brain prefers to use what it knows.
- Negativity dominates the brain.
- The brain does not think well under stress.

What are the one or two things in this listing that you notice about your own brain function? What are some of the tips from the reading you can employ to strengthen your ability to chose what your brain does? Write one or two things that you can do that will help you make good brain choices.

_____

_____

2. Think about the last time you got trapped in your Pain Cycle and were full into your reactive coping. Write down some key words that remind you of the elements of this memory and then write down a few of the emotions you felt in the situation or some of the reactive things you did.

_____

_____

3. If you are willing, now try a simple meditation exercise. Chose one Bible verse that is particularly comforting to you. For one minute, read the verse slowly three times out loud. For two minutes more, close your eyes and contemplate what the verse is saying to you. End your time with prayer. After you are done, notice how you feel about the situation and the words you have written above about your last Pain Cycle experience. Did the meditation help you reduce your stress or anxiety? How do you think you could use this meditation exercise the next time you are in your Pain Cycle? Write down a few of your ideas.

_____

_____

The Four Steps

Now it is time to get down to serious and intentional mindfulness work using the four steps. We must admit that we always find ourselves feeling a little foolish when we show these four steps to people, because they are so simple and seem so obvious. Yet these steps give people the mindfulness leverage they need in order to make the change in the moment of truth from the Pain Cycle to the Peace Cycle.

> ## THE FOUR STEPS
>
> 1. Say what you feel.
> 2. Say what you normally do.
> 3. Say the truth.
> 4. Say what you will do differently.

When do you do these four steps?

You do these four steps when you notice that you are emotionally disregulated and into your Pain Cycle. Do not be discouraged when you are first starting this work, because many times you will realize your emotional disregulation and Pain Cycle in retrospect after hours have passed. No worries and no judgment on yourself. As soon as you realize that you were or are in your Pain Cycle, that is the time to employ these four steps. As you do more and more work using this mindfulness trick, you will realize that you are noticing when you are in your Pain Cycle much quicker in the process.

1. Say what you feel.

Step 1 is to say out loud how you are actually feeling when you are in your Pain Cycle. You should review how you normally feel by looking back at Exercise 3, page 28. This first step is essential because, in the midst of your Pain Cycle, you will be tempted to say things like "I feel angry" or "I feel frustrated" or "I feel like leaving." Remember that all these phrases are representative of what you are *doing*

115

right now and your reactive coping with how you feel. It may be true that you are angry, but you are acting that way because you have had one of your primary emotions pushed concerning your identity and sense of safety. These primary emotions are more likely to be things like feeling unloved, unwanted, controlled, and so on. These feelings are the ones that you most likely feel again and again and are related to your past programming around identity and sense of safety and not only from your interactions with the current situation or relationship.

In many ways, this step is about *actualizing* your real feelings. Instead of confusing your most basic and primary emotions with reactive coping such as anger, guilt, shame, controlling, or escaping, you are accurately naming the true heart of how you feel. Often you do not realize that these basic emotional buttons around identity and safety have been pushed until you call them out loud. Remember also that you should always start first with the words that you have listed as feelings in your Pain Cycle.

It is not that you cannot feel anything different, but when you are emotionally disregulated, there is a 90 percent chance that what you feel is closely related to these primary emotions you have already listed. How do we know this? Remember that the brain is likely to use the emotions that it already knows well. In many ways, your emotional disregulation is preprogrammed. You will find, when you feel primary emotions, that they will overwhelmingly be the same primary emotions.

When we say, "Say what you feel," we truly want you to say it out loud. Remember that your brain is able to think through a huge number of thoughts, emotions, and actions in just one second. It is no wonder that it is confusing when you are in your Pain Cycle and trying to name what you feel. You will be tempted to go with the thought, emotion, or behavior you are doing. Again, saying what you feel *out loud* will likely slow down your processing by moving the thoughts to various parts of your brain. When you finally hear the feeling you are saying, your brain is much more likely to pay careful attention to what you are saying.

Whether you are with others or by yourself, you may feel silly saying what you feel out loud. Yet this is exactly what we want you to do. It will likely only take you one to two minutes to go through all four steps when you are headed to Peace Cycle regulation. We promise that, although someone else may not initially realize what you are doing, he or she will notice the change in direction you take from being emotionally reactive to being loving and trustworthy in your actions. Even if you are by yourself, say what you feel aloud. Saying it out loud slows you down and stacks the cards in your favor, enabling you to actually change something that you are feeling and head in a different direction.

Whatever you listed in Exercise 3, page 28, as the way you feel, get those words programmed into your brain. You don't have to invent or look for how you feel every time you are in your Pain Cycle; it will likely already be closely aligned with the feelings you have listed. Getting it into your head means memorizing those feeling words and practicing them over and over again through step 1.

2. Say what you normally do.

Next, it is time to do some prediction of behavior. If you look back at Exercise 4, page 39, you will find those actions and behaviors that you normally take in reactive coping with the feelings you feel. Again, these actions and behaviors are predictable and you will be doing some version of this coping 90 percent of the time when you are under stress or in a relational conflict.

When we say, "Say what you normally do," we again intend you to say it out loud. This not only slows down the processing in your brain but it also starts the process of learning your "tricks" in terms of old-self behaviors. When you have the courage to say what you normally do in the way of coping or actions, you are actually predicting what you would do if left unchecked and remembering what you have done in the past. You know that these actions and coping have not been good for you and have not been good for your relationships because these are the actions that violate love and trustworthiness and do destructive things to you and others. When you say them out loud, you are really confessing you once again have the potential to take those destructive actions and the very things that have not worked for you in the past.

When you have the courage to name these "tricks" to your brain in a format where you can hear them and think about them differently, your cognition gives you leverage to change. Naming your destructive actions in your Pain Cycle before you do them actually gives your brain the time and space it needs to make a decision: *Do I really want to take these actions?* You will find that if you slow yourself down with this kind of awareness, then the overwhelming majority of the time you will resist the pattern of the Pain Cycle and chose to continue with the steps.

By doing these first two steps, you have done half the work in Paul's direction to us. By being "renewed in the spirit of your mind," you have done the mindfulness work to take off the old self. You still have work to do in steps three and four, but chances are, you are beginning to feel that you have the power to choose something new as an alternative to the Pain Cycle.

3. Say the truth.

Do you remember how, in Day 2, we talked about the children of Israel under Joshua decisively crossing the Jordan River into the Promised Land? Here, in step 3, is where you will do the hard work of "crossing the Jordan." It is in this step where you will feel some emotional relief from the pain that originates in your identity and safety. Say the truth about yourself that you identified in Exercise 8, page 59.

Dealing with the painful emotions that you normally feel when you are dis-regulated means you are not just dealing with the current situation but you are also dealing with the emotional baggage of all the times when you have felt these feelings in the past. No matter how long these feelings have been present and how accommodating you have been to these feelings about your identity and safety, it is time to acknowledge that they represent a lie about who you are and your ability to be safe.

You may feel unloved. It is a lie.

You may feel worthless. It is a lie.

You may feel like a failure. It is a lie.

You may feel that every situation you are in is unsafe. It is a lie.

When you say the truth (again, say it out loud), you are actively rejecting the lie and utilizing focus, hopefulness, and positivity to change your brain. You are much more loved, more worthy, more empowered to do good and strong enough to persist and thrive in situations that are challenging. Taking this step into the truth, and remembering the hard work you did on Day 2, means that you are actively confronting the lie and proclaiming to yourself the intention to live in the truth. This kind of truth, like any truth, has the power to set you free from the old self.

When you say the truth, you are not denying the feelings in the Pain Cycle but instead are actively confronting them with the message you chose to parent yourself with. These are words that God and the ones who love you best would be in full agreement with. You step into the river and, with faithfulness, you walk to the other side and look the pain about your identity and safety eye to eye. This confrontation is the opportunity to give yourself the gift of true identity and real empowerment. It not only acknowledges what is true about you, but it also provides the opportunity to replace the lies that you currently feel.

How can you make these truths more than just words? Remember how God encouraged the people to get the truth of the law into their hearts. He said, "These words that I command you today shall be on your heart. You shall teach them diligently to your children, and shall talk of them when you sit in your house, and when you walk by the way, and when you lie down, and when you rise. You shall write them on the doorposts of your house and on your gates" (*Deuteronomy 6:6-9*). So by following this model, you get your truth into yourself by writing it down and repeating it to yourself throughout the day. You become *relentless* in teaching yourself the truth about your identity and safety. It is that important.

If you take the responsibility to teach the truth to yourself and embrace it throughout your days, instead of looking to others to reassure you about your identity and safety, you will see a profound difference in the power of the Pain Cycle. You will notice that you are much less prone to being in the Pain Cycle and, when you get into it, you are much quicker in getting back into the Peace Cycle.

When we were young in our faith, we memorized scriptures in order to encourage our walk of discipleship. One of the key verses we memorized was this one: "This Book of the Law shall not depart from your mouth, but you shall meditate on it day and night, so that you may be careful to do according to all that is written in it. For then you will make your way prosperous, and then you will have good success" (*Joshua 1:8*). You can apply this verse to telling yourself the truth.

It's not that the truths you should be telling yourself are Scripture. But they are God-approved messages. All truth is God's truth.

If you know, agree with, and meditate on this new script written on your heart, you will find that you have success in emotionally regulating yourself even when you are in the toughest situations and relationships. It will take practice and discipline to do over and over again. But as you utilize the truth in step 3, you will likely notice that some of the tension will leave your body. You will notice that your breathing becomes more regular and fuller and you let yourself give a heavy sigh of relief. When you see these signs, you will realize you have crossed the Jordan into a new territory right in the moment of truth when your behavior could have stayed in the old Pain Cycle.

We want to give a warning about step 3 and emotional regulation.

Sometimes individuals will be working the four steps and will say something like this: "How do I feel? I feel worthless, unappreciated, and like a failure. When I feel this way, what do I normally do? I normally get angry, negative, and attack! What is the truth? The truth is that people don't care about me and don't love me. The truth is that life is terrible!"

In other words, often we are still emotionally disregulated to the point where we are not ready to talk about the truth but instead want to use this step to comment on how our Pain Cycle is justified. *This is not what step 3 is about!*

120

If you find yourself saying the four steps in the fashion above, simply circle back to step 1 and say again how you feel. Start over as many times as it takes to let the truth about your identity and safety sink into your emotions. It may take saying the four steps two, three or even four times to get to a place where you are living in your Peace Cycle. No worries and no judgment on yourself. Keep your focus, and your emotions will eventually be regulated with the truth.

4. Say what you will do differently.

When you feel the truth taking hold, you will likely find yourself empowered to make a different behavioral choice. Instead of reactively coping with those destructive feelings, you will be enabled by the truth to look at what you can do differently. The specific behaviors and actions you choose for yourself are found in Exercise 10, page 92. Take a look at those actions and behaviors you identified and try to imprint them into your mind's memory.

Remember also that these actions you have chosen have the potential to always be winners when it comes to difficult situations and relationships. They are winners because, when you take the actions, they produce a sense of intimacy and truth. We will speak more about the value of these new actions and how they can change us even more in the next section. But right now, we want you to realize that saying what you will do differently does not just stop with identification; you will find that you are most effective in the four steps when you just don't say what you will do differently but you say and then do it differently.

When you do steps three and four, you have now completed the circle that Paul is suggesting to us in Ephesians 4. The "renewing of your mind," or spiritual mindfulness, has led you to put on the new self. Steps 1 and 2 guide you in taking off the old-self Pain Cycle; steps 3 and 4 guide you to put on the new-self Peace Cycle. This is how the model we are suggesting is really a discipleship model of how to be more conformed to the image of Jesus. The more you practice the four steps, the more you will find yourself transformed into His image.

EXERCISE 13
Practicing the Four Steps

1. Think again about the last time you were in your Pain Cycle and review the situation in your mind. See if you can recapture some of the emotions in that situation. Fill in the four steps below. Remember to use your Pain and Peace Cycles from exercises 5 and 11, pages 43 and 96.

When I was in that situation, I felt _____

_____.

When I was in that situation, what I did was _____

_____.

The truth about me in that situation was _____

_____.

What I should have done differently was _____

_____.

2. Imagine how you could put the four steps to use the next time you find yourself in the Pain Cycle. Take some time to commit your Pain and Peace Cycles to memory as well as to memorize the four steps. If helpful, take pictures of your Pain and Peace Cycles as well as the four steps on your phone for easy reference. Where else can you put these cycles and illustrations that would make it easier to commit to memory? Make note of these things to yourself.

_____

_____

3. Be on the lookout for your next experience in the Pain Cycle. Either in the moment or afterward, try out the four steps. Return to this page afterward and record some of your experience of utilizing the four steps for the first time.

_____

_____

Living into the Experience and Practicing, Practicing, Practicing

The four steps will serve you well in slowing you down in the speedway of the Pain Cycle and enabling you to perceive how to move in the other direction in terms of your Peace Cycle. You may need to slow yourself down physiologically with some calming exercises such as breathing, relaxation, or meditation before you do the four steps, but the mindfulness practiced out loud will work for you an amazing percentage of the time.

When you get to that fourth step, it is important to put flesh on the bone of your Peace Cycle by actually doing what you say you intend to do. For instance, I (Terry) say my four steps in this manner: "I feel unloved, unwanted, and like a failure. What I normally do when I feel this way is withdraw and shame myself, perform, or get angry. The truth about me is that I am loved, wanted, and 'man enough' to do things that are needed. What I will do differently is stay connected to the issues and nurture those around me while I value myself."

It is now essential for me to move to staying connected with those around me, nurturing them, and actually valuing myself. I live into this experience by saying the truth to myself again and again and reminding myself how God has used me productively in the past even though I am imperfect. I move into a relationship—at work, at home, or over the phone—and connect with someone and talk to them, being careful to encourage, listen, and appreciate them.

When I actually do the fourth step and don't just name it, the experience confirms in me the truths that I have said out loud. The connection tells me that I am a lovable and wanted person, while my nurturing of myself and others assures me that I am doing the most important thing in life well.

This living into the fourth step means that you do the action you are saying you will do. It will put a exclamation point to your new-self work and settle you even more in the Pain Cycle. It's like what James said: "Be doers of the word, and not hearers only, deceiving yourselves. For if anyone is a hearer of the word and not a doer, he is like a man who looks intently at his natural face in a mirror. For he looks at himself and goes away and at once forgets what he was like. But the one who looks into the perfect law, the law of liberty, and perseveres, being no hearer who forgets but a doer who acts, he will be blessed in his doing" (*James 1:22-25*).

Experience in the Peace Cycle is like food and water to your growth in the new self. As you become a "doer" in your step 4, you will see that it becomes easier and easier for you to turn to your Peace Cycle when you start getting enticed by your Pain Cycle. Remember, your brain is a great learner, and as you build experience into your four steps, you will see the neural pathways develop and your comfort level in the Peace Cycle increase. If you just say your four steps, you will gain a little insight and you will see small changes. But if you add *doing* your forth step experientially, you will see the big new-self changes you crave.

One more issue concerning your four steps: the more you practice, the more you will see results. If you look at your pain and Peace Cycles and go over your four steps ten times within twelve days, you will find that you have your Pain and Peace Cycles memorized. If you practice fifteen times over twenty days, you will begin to notice that you can easily look at times when you fell into your Pain Cycle and, in retrospect within a couple of hours, will easily be able to recognize what you were doing and how you could have implemented the four steps. But if you practice the four steps twenty-three to twenty-five times within one month, there will be at least one time when you are deep into your old-self Pain Cycle behavior and you think, *Wait, I know what I am doing! I am in my Pain Cycle! I need to do the four steps!* If you follow your intention and do the four steps, you will likely have success at moving yourself from the pain you were feeling and the destructive trajectory of your reactive coping to new-self Peace Cycle behavior. It will be success in the moment of truth.

Remember that the brain is most likely to repeat what it knows, so if you practice the new-self truths and actions more, you will continue to see change and growth. The point is, if you use the skill that you have learned in the four steps, you can see the new self emerge and the old self become less and less dominating.

Will your Pain Cycle disappear?

Unfortunately, it will not. Your stuff will remain your stuff for many years to come because it is part of your wiring and original program.

But we can assure you that with practice your old self can never be dominating and unchallenged. As we often say, you may fall in the ditch of the Pain Cycle, but if you practice your four steps, you will always know how to climb out of the ditch and get into your Peace Cycle.

EXERCISE 14
Committing to Using the Four Steps

1. Read and meditate on the following passage: "Those who live according to the flesh set their minds on the things of the flesh, but those who live according to the Spirit set their minds on the things of the Spirit. For to set the mind on the flesh is death, but to set the mind on the Spirit is life and peace" (*Romans 8:5-6*).

2. Now think about how you would like to apply and practice the four steps. Remember that practicing ten times within twelve days will result in memorization learning; fifteen times within twenty days will result in ability to apply the four steps in retrospect easily; twenty-three to twenty-five times in thirty days will result in an ability to interrupt your Pain Cycle while it is happening using the four steps. What commitment would you like to make to yourself about applying the four steps in the coming weeks? Write this commitment down.

_____

_____

A Day to Prepare for Your Moments of Truth

"Since we are surrounded by so great a cloud of witnesses," says the writer of Hebrews, "let us also lay aside every weight, and sin which clings so closely, and let us run with endurance the race that is set before us, looking to Jesus, the founder and perfecter of our faith, who for the joy that was set before him endured the cross, despising the shame, and is seated at the right hand of the throne of God" (*Hebrews 12:1-2*).

You are now on the athletic field of life. A great cloud of witnesses—all the past saints—are in the stands watching and cheering for you. Jesus, the author and perfecter of your faith and Peace Cycle, is out on the field with you as your coach. And here is your moment of truth. Will you follow the way of the Pain Cycle, or will you go the way of the new-self Peace Cycle?

This has been a day of learning how to build the muscle to run your race in your moment of truth. Remember, you have a good set of skills and leverage to negotiate the race. You have people who have run the race before and are cheering for you. And you have Jesus coaching you in your quest to become a new self in His image. You were made for this moment, and we know you will have success!

For Reflection

1. In order to work with your brain in developing the new self, say your four steps out loud. This may feel awkward, especially the first few times you give them a try. So start now to get used to it. Say your four steps out loud with a friend or a group.

2. In the exercises from this chapter, you were encouraged to think of times you were in your Pain Cycle. Has an incident of your Pain Cycle happened this week or in the last few days? Think about this incident and share it with a friend or a group. Then, in the presence of the friend or group, say your four steps using the following prompts:

• In this situation, I felt _____.

• When I felt this way, I normally do or did _____.

• The truth about me is _____.

• In this situation, I should have done differently by _____.

After you are finished, ask your friend or the group for feedback and report to them your own analysis.

3. Was there a time after you read this chapter that you were able to put some ideas to use in terms of working with your brain, mindfulness, or doing the four steps? If so, discuss your work with a friend or group.

4. Talk with a friend or a group about your commitment to practicing the Peace Cycle (Exercise 14, page 125). Be sure to ask for support and prayers as you work to fulfill your commitment to practice.

DAY FIVE

— ◆ ◆ ◆ ◆ ◆ —

You and "Us"

It had been an exciting few days with Jesus in the feeding of the five thousand and His walking on water. The crowd sought after Jesus, looking to see what He might do next, like groupies who could not get enough of the excitement and the party. It was an amazing time to be in the presence of this kind of rock star. The problem was, Jesus knew that these folks were not committed followers and He was not there for their entertainment. So He made it clear to them that His purpose was to show the reality of God being in their midst and to create new relationship. He said, "I am the bread of life; whoever comes to me shall not hunger, and whoever believes in me shall never thirst" (*John 6:35*).

This was upsetting to some people, who pointed out that He was just the son of Mary and Joseph. There was nothing special about Him.

As if to twist their noses, Jesus repeated not only that He was bread from heaven but also said that if anyone believed in Him and ate the bread (His flesh), then he or she would live eternally.

Now His critics were enraged. "How can this man give us his flesh to eat?" they asked (*John 6:52*).

Jesus did not stop. Instead, He poured gasoline on the fire of the others' rage. He insisted, "Truly, truly, I say to you, unless you eat the flesh of the Son of Man and drink his blood, you have no life in you. Whoever feeds on my flesh and drinks my blood has eternal life, and I will raise him up on the last day" (*John 6:53-54*).

The people of Capernaum, the crowds who were following, and even the disciples who knew Him best were all stunned by the brutal image of consuming the body and blood of Jesus. It is one thing to be a follower of a rock star and watch the party; it is quite another to consume every part of another human being and make His substance—His body and blood—intermingle with your own.

Why did Jesus say such a thing? Even many of His disciples confronted Him with this question, saying that what He had said was a hard thing to accept.

Yet Jesus said it clearly to them, without watering down the message. Belief—true belief—means that you do not just come to see Jesus and hang out with Him; it means that you make His substance come alive in you. This is the kind of life and faith that saves.

It was as harsh a message then as it is now, and the crowds departed. So Jesus looked at the Twelve and said, "How about you guys? You want to leave too?"

Peter, as a true believer, answered, "Lord, to whom shall we go? You have the words of eternal life, and we have believed, and have come to know, that you are the Holy One of God" (*John 6:68-69*).

Communion

In Western culture, many of us live with the idea that our individuality rules supreme; our identity and our sense of safety are under our control and up to our choice. But Jesus openly challenges our individuality. What in essence He is saying in John 6 is this: "If you believe in me, you must become wholeheartedly committed to me. You must take in my very substance and intermingle it with your substance. In every part of your being, I will be present and in my being you will be present." Essentially, He is telling us that we become joined as one. We are no longer an individual but rather an "us" in union with Jesus.

This does not mean that we become God. We still have our individuality intact the same way Jesus is the Christ. But, just like two people become an "us" in marriage, so we become joined in an "us" relationship with the living God.

Our individuality is not obliterated, but our "us" relationship with Christ now becomes the more important mission and the more important identity.

Of course, this is what Jesus was saying in a more pleasing and easier analogy: "I am the vine; you are the branches. Whoever abides in me and I in him, he it is that bears much fruit, for apart from me you can do nothing" (*John 15:5*). Jesus is in us and we are in Him. We are in a new "us" relationship with Him where His mission and heart becomes our mission and heart. This is the most radical of all the radical things God did through Jesus Christ: He made a way for us to become intertwined with God to have a part in His resurrection, life, mission, and hope. We often partake of communion and the Eucharist remembering the body and blood of Christ. Our "us" with the living Christ is actually the true communion as we remember that Christ is the vine; we are the branches; that He is in us and we are in Him.

"Us" is an interesting concept. In relationships, we usually think of two communicating one with another, compromising with one another, and doing good and helpful acts toward one another. An "us" relationship is a bit different in that two individuals produce a third identity, a "what we are together" identity. In this idea, "us" is not quite like me or quite like you; it is a combination of the two of us. In our "us" with Christ, there is the Christ, me, and what we are together—the body of Christ.

But while our new "us" with Christ brings us resurrection and eternal life, it also means that we share in the sufferings of Christ. In our new "us" relationship, we have to learn the process of "dying to self" and "crucifying" our old-self behaviors. Our relationship with the living God requires us to reach deeper and deeper to take off our old self so that we can better fit the new-self mission in relationship to Christ.

We are often asked, "How do I maintain and grow this change I am learning?" On this Day 5 of the work, you need to know that if any of this is going to stick with you, it will have to continue as a way of life. You have had the courage to reckon with yourself and your pain, recognize the truth about your identity

131

and safety, and put together a map of peace to pursue, and you have started practicing taking off the old and putting on the new. But today you must learn that it has to become a way of life. In other words, you will have to live out Day 5 and recapitulate the work you have done in this book throughout your lifetime.

The most essential element in maintaining this drive is for you to see your "us" relationship and communion with Jesus as living and breathing. You are not trying to change by yourself. In Jesus, you have a companion who knows every part of you and every fiber of your motivation. Jesus already knows the areas where you need to change and grow. As you are in Him and He is in you, He will point out those areas that need work and be a helper to you as you cooperate with the work of the Spirit to make yourself fit better with Him. If we have Jesus, the communion and "us" with Him guides us to keep working toward real change and gives us motivation and power to work in our truth, peace, and four steps.

EXERCISE 15
Using Your "Us-ness" with Christ to Move to Your New Self

1. Think about the statement in John 15 where Christ says, "I am the vine; you are the branches. Whoever abides in me and I in him, he it is that bears much fruit, for apart from me you can do nothing." What are some ways that you benefit positively from being in a close "us" relationships with Christ? What are some harder realities that you must share in because of your "us-ness" with Christ? Make some notes of both of these ideas.

_____

_____

2. As you look at some of the things you listed above, both positive and more difficult, what does it do to your outlook of moving from the old self to the new self? Do these things make you more or less motivated to work on your Pain Cycle? Write some of your thoughts down.

_____

_____

Connection and Community

The second thing we can do to keep change moving in our lives through Day 5 and beyond is to connect in significant relationships.

We have already discussed the fact that we were built to be relationally dependent and build trustworthiness, but really relationships are essential to our very identity. In his book *I and Thou*, theologian-philosopher Martin Buber says that there is no way for us to know ourselves as individuals without another person reflecting back to us interpretations about our ideas, actions, and physical being.[11] For instance, I can think I have a good idea, but unless others around me confirm that the idea has potential to work or help me put the idea into play where it does work, I cannot know for sure whether the idea is sound. It is in the context of others that I can find the truth about the legitimacy of what I am thinking.

My understanding of my identity and being is dependent upon my relating to the environment and to the people around me. Relationships are the mirror I hold up in front of myself. But this mirror not only helps me understand what I look like physically; this mirror helps me understand my ideas, concepts, thoughts, and emotions at deeper levels. Others give me the context needed to interpret concepts about my identity and safety. Without them, I have no way to understand myself and the world.

The point we are making is this: relationships are imperative for self- understanding. You cannot successfully go it alone, simply because you do not have the interaction needed for self-understanding.

But there is also another part essential in this *I and Thou* relationship. Buber also makes it clear to us that we grow as we interact with other. As we interact, we learn more and more things about our identities as well as encounter other challenges in learning how to trust and relate. These revelations and challenges will move us in one of two directions: we will either grow to become more loving and more trustworthy with one another or we will be driven into isolation, individuality, and stagnation by ourselves.

Nothing will challenge you more to change than when you are connected to relationships. Jesus connected the two essential commandments together: "You shall love the Lord your God with all your heart and with all your soul and with all your mind. This is the great and first commandment. And a second is like it: You shall love your neighbor as yourself. On these two commandments depend all the Law and the Prophets" (*Matthew 22:37-40*). In other words, the way you love God should end up being reflected in the way you love others, and vice versa.

James makes this point strongly when he states that no one can love God and let his or her brother go in need. Faith in God without loving others is dead faith (*James 2:14-17*). So it is with growth. We cannot say we are interested in growing spiritually and in our "us" relationship with Christ and then isolate from others or hold on to our old ways when we deal with others in relationships. Becoming more like Jesus in our new self demands that we also make growth and change real in our current relationships. If we do one without the other, what good is our change? To paraphrase James, spiritual growth that doesn't result in relational growth is dead.

When we enter an "us" relationship with Christ, we quickly find that certain parts of our being and actions do not fit and need to change to work in the relationship with the holy God. The same is true of relationships with people. Parts of our personhoods, personalities, and the way we behave do not always fit. In order to be loving and trustworthy, the relationships demand that we make accommodations, modifications, and changes in ourselves. Relationships point us toward the areas where we need to grow, and that kind of growth then gets actively reflected in our relationship with Jesus.

Sharon's mother, Genevieve, was a wonderful woman in many ways and was courageous, positive, and resourceful. She also had a drinking problem. In her pain of loss and lack of safety, she escaped into too much wine and too much numbing out. But then, as she grew older and in need of care because of Alzheimer's disease, she had less and less access to alcohol and so rarely drank.

I (Terry) loved Genevieve deeply and strove to do my fair share of the caregiving. So one afternoon when I received a message from Genevieve's personal care facility that she was acting strangely, I was there within minutes. Because I had worked with an aging population, I knew the telltale signs of a stroke and I believed she was in the midst of a minor incident. After she was rushed to the hospital, her neurologist met me there and examined her. The doctor's suspicions confirmed my fears that she was in the midst of a stroke. Immediately the hospital staff swung into action.

Meanwhile, I went to a waiting area, where Sharon later joined me. We discussed the implications of Genevieve's future care and the probable demands that would come our way. After about half an hour, the neurologist came into our room, holding some lab results. She said, "Fortunately she is not having a stroke. Her blood work indicates that she is drunk."

I was furious at my mother-in-law. Sharon and I had worked so hard to provide loving care for Genevieve, and here she was in a state of Alzheimer's still figuring out ways to drink! I got her in the car and gave her a piece of my mind, saying that she could care less about how she was ruining our lives.

She could care less about how she was ruining our lives.

I still have these words echoing in my head fifteen years after I yelled them.

Here was my mother-in-law, who gave her life to love, raise, and care for her family despite the suicide of her husband and the deaths of two of her sons. Furthermore, she loved and nurtured me like a son when I entered the family as a young man. And here I was, yelling at her that she was ruining my life.

I thought I was loving Genevieve because I was a good caregiver. The reality, however, is that I was not a good lover at all and had far to go in getting rid of my old-self Pain Cycle. The relationship and God were both pointing me to how unloving and untrustworthy I was in my role of taking care of Genevieve. I received a terrible gift that revealed to me where I needed to work on my Pain Cycle more and how I needed to become much more nurturing.

This is what real connection will do for you: it will point out the areas in your Pain Cycle where you have to change.

But of course, pointing out what needs to change is only part of the story in connection with relationships. Just as in our relationship with Christ, connections with other people provide us with the food and water of love and trustworthiness we need to flourish. Our relationships hold the resource to encourage, appreciate, care for, share, exhort, connect, and hold fast in our times when we need people on our side. We are not alone, and family, friends, and others provide "us" relationships that keep us going in healthy and strong ways. As one biblical writer states, "Let us consider how to stir up one another to love and good works, not neglecting to meet together, as is the habit of some, but encouraging one another, and all the more as you see the Day drawing near" (*Hebrews 10:24-25*).

Many of us will look around at our relationships and think, *My friends (or my family) could really benefit from getting out of their Pain Cycles.* And many of us would be more than willing to show them where they need to change!

While it may be appropriate on a rare occasion to point out someone else's pain, by and large, doing so is an avoidance of your responsibility to change. If you are wise enough to see that some of your friends or family members are in their Pain Cycles, then you should be wise enough to realize that it is pushing your buttons and putting you into your own Pain Cycle.

Here is what we recommend: keep your focus on moving yourself to peace instead of focusing on what others should do. In doing this, you will find some positive outcomes. First, you will be actively working on yourself and find that you will like yourself much more in your Peace Cycle than in your Pain Cycle or than when you are commenting on others' Pain Cycles. Second, if you work on yourself and move into new-self behavior, you will likely find that nurturing, self-valuing, balanced give-and-take, and reliably connecting systemically produce change in others. Finally, you will find that focusing on your own issues keeps you aware of the log in your own eye instead of the speck in someone else's eye (Matthew 7:4-5). Never underestimate the good that can come from staying out of a judgmental stance.

Communion with Christ and connection with one another should drive you toward the reality of community. You cannot live out your change from old-self behavior to new-self behavior in your head but rather must live it out in the context of real relationships. It is popular to say, "It takes a village to raise a child." In actuality, it takes a village to grow and nurture any human being. It is only in the context of many relationships that we not only gain the love and encouragement we need but also experience the growth needed to become loving and trustworthy nurturers of one another.

Amazing things happen when people love and grow together. You have likely seen this reality in a small group, family, or church. But chances are, you have seen—even in the same contexts—groups, families, and churches that are selfish, deceitful, and conceited with one another.

It is wonderful when things work well. But this is not the truest test of the community. It is precisely when the community is full of individuals who are in their Pain Cycles, and who nevertheless find the ability to emotionally regulate and come together to be loving and trustworthy, that you find community at its best.

Think back to the devastation of 9/11. Think about how people who were locked in the pain and grief of loss came together in a real, albeit brief, stance of love and compassion for one another.

When we go into a community of relationships, "us" is anything but easy. But this difficulty runs us into our Pain Cycles. Our Pain Cycles then run us into the opportunities to emotionally regulate and move to our new-self Peace Cycles. Our Peace Cycles next enable us to be the kind of community that nurtures, loves, and is safe. We do not just need community when it does right by us; we need community so we can learn to be right and at peace. As Paul said, "If there is any encouragement in Christ, any comfort from love, any participation in the Spirit, any affection and sympathy, complete my joy by being of the same mind, having the same love, being in full accord and of one mind" (*Philippians 2:1-2*).

EXERCISE 16
Living Out Your New Self in Community

1. Think about the one to five people in your life you can count on, not only to be your friend(s), but also to be honest with you and to mentor you when you need help with change. Write the name or names of these people down. Do these people know your Pain and Peace Cycles? Tell these people of your desire to practice taking off the old self and putting on the new self by sharing your Pain and Peace Cycles and the four steps. These are the people who will likely serve as your encouragers, nurturers, and mentors in this process.

_____

_____

2. Think about the people, groups, co-workers, or fellow believers who serve as your community. Think of this community as your "us" grouping along with Christ. What are the current issues or difficulties that are occurring in your community? As you think about your own Pain Cycle in the midst of these current issues, are you interacting with people more out of your pain or more out of your peace? If you have times in your pain, write down some situations and contexts where you could use your four steps to be more loving and trustworthy using your Peace Cycle.

_____

_____

_____

_____

A Day of Engaging the New Self Today and Forever

In January 2009, U.S. Airways flight 1549 smashed into a flock of geese just after leaving LaGuardia Airport in New York. Both engines were put out of commission and the plane was hopelessly crippled and going down. Everyone aboard, including the crew, felt panic at the thought that they were all going down. The pilots immediately knew the seriousness of the situation.

The pilot, Chesley B. "Sully" Sullenberger, and the copilot did not let their "first natures" of panic and fear control them but instead took control of the plane and started working through the procedures to restart the engines. Within seconds, Sully had communicated with LaGuardia on landing options and, step by step, assessed the options of what he could do to land the plane. The reality became clear within seconds—the engines would not start. Sully made the decision to land the plane on the Hudson River. He and his copilot continued to work through checklists to prepare the aircraft for the water landing, while the flight attendants in the back of the plane prepared the passengers. With unbelievable skill, Sully guided the plane down, reducing the forward motion to a survivable crash speed while keeping it high enough to keep the plane flying as long as he needed it to. The crew ditched the plane in the Hudson River, and all 155 people on board the plane survived.

Was it a miracle, as many people called it? Sullenberger and his crew said over and over again that their training kicked in as soon as they realized the seriousness of the situation. They had been trained to develop a "second nature" on which they could depend by going through those types of scenarios many times in flight simulators that gave them the practice, skill, and expertise to land the plane. If they had done what just came naturally to their first nature, there would have been panic and likely 155 fewer souls here on earth. But because they had trained their second nature adequately, they immediately had brain pathways that could respond and solve the problem. Their second nature had now become as natural as, and even more powerful than, the first. A miracle? Yes, but it was a miracle of taking off the old and natural and putting on the new.

You stand at the precipice of the new self. You have the knowledge, insight, and skill to enter into it, but it is a matter of working out the mechanics in real life. The more you practice, the more your communion and "us-ness" with the living God will come alive. The more you practice, the more your relationships with other people will become real, intimate, and deep. And the more you practice, the more you will find that you are in the position to lead, guide, and even save your community. Never underestimate how God can use one soul willing to live out the new self in the midst of community.

We have every confidence that you can live out this new self and practice your way to the miracle.

For Reflection

1. After Jesus's resurrection, He had an encounter with Peter by the sea where He asked him the famous series of "Do you love me?" questions. After Jesus told Peter the type of death by which he would be martyred, Peter's eye wandered to the disciple John. "When Peter saw him, he said to Jesus, 'Lord, what about this man?' Jesus said to him, 'If it is my will that he remain until I come, what is that to you? You follow me!' " (John 21:21-22). We all get focused on what we think others should do and the changes we think they should make instead of focusing on our own needed change. What can you do to focus on your own Pain and Peace Cycles and your four steps? How could you resist the temptation of focusing on others' needed changes? Discuss these ideas with a friend or a group.

2. There are times when each of us and our relationships serve the larger community. These moments can be ones when God uses us in a particular way that makes something essential happen. These are moments when you serve as a hinge of history that swings God's plan into action, and these things can be either large and public acts or small and personal ones. What are some ways you currently are or could be a person who makes a difference in your community and relationships? How does being in your Peace Cycle enhance this opportunity? Discuss these ideas with a friend or group.

3. Think about your most recent work in dealing with your Pain Cycle and your four steps. Take some time and review your Pain and Peace Cycles surrounding your recent experience with a friend or a group.

4. Evaluate how you have done thus far in learning your Pain and Peace Cycles and the four steps. What changes are you noticing? What signs are encouraging or discouraging to you? What areas of this model are the most troubling or difficult for you? Where are you having success? Share your evaluation with your friend or a group.

5. Relationships and community are essential to the process of practicing new-self behavior. If sharing with a friend or a group has been helpful to you in reviewing these "For Reflection" suggestions, you might consider continue meeting three or four more times together over the next several weeks, reporting on your experiences with the Pain and Peace Cycles as well as doing your four steps in the moments of emotional disregulation. See encouragement and be an encourager in your community.

NOTES

1. Emotional disregulation occurs when negative emotions crowd out everything positive in your brain and lead you to take destructive or regrettable actions.

2. Henri J. M. Nouwen, *The Life of the Beloved: Spiritual Living in a Secular World* (New York: Crossroad, 1992).

3. Primo Levi, *Survival in Auschwitz: The Nazi Assault on Humanity*, trans. Stuart Woolf (New York: Touchstone, 1986), 40.

4. Maya Angelou, quoted at goodreads, http://www.goodreads.com/quotes/3759-courage-is-the-most-important-of-all-the-virtues-because.

5. Maya Angelou, plenary speech at the seventeenth annual Family Therapy Networker (Washington, D.C., 1993).

6. Maya Angelou, quoted at goodreads, http://www.goodreads.com/quotes/184013-i-don-t-trust-people-who-don-t-love-themselves-and-tell.

7. Tanya Lewis, "Human Brain Microchip Is 9000 Times Faster than a PC," Live Science, May 2, 2014, http://www.livescience.com/45304-human-brain-microchip-9000-times-faster-than-pc.html; Jeff Bollow, "How Fast Is Your Brain?" The Phenomenal Experience, http://thephenomenalexperience.com/content/how-fast-is-your-brain.

8. Alexander Atkins, "Tag Archives: How Many Words in the Average Person's Vocabulary?" Atkins Bookshelf, July 16, 2013, https://atkinsbookshelf.wordpress.com/tag/how-many-words-in-the-average-persons-vocabulary/.

9. Rick Hanson, "Overcoming the Negativity Bias," Rick Hanson, Ph.D., February 26, 2014, https://www.rickhanson.net/overcoming-negativity-bias/.

10. John Gottman, *Why Marriages Succeed or Fail: And How to Make Yours Last* (New York: Simon & Schuster, 1995).

11. Martin Buber, *I and Thou*, trans. Ronald Gregor Smith (1937; reprint, New York: Scribner, 2010).

About the Authors

Terry Hargrave, Ph.D., is nationally recognized for his pioneering work with intergenerational families. Dr. Hargrave has authored numerous professional articles and eleven books, including *The Essential Humility of Marriage, Honoring the Third Identity in Couple Therapy, Restoration Therapy*, and *5 Days to a New Marriage*.

Terry has presented nationally and internationally on the concepts and processes of family and marriage restoration as well as aging. His work has been featured in several national magazines and newspapers as well as *ABC News 20/20, Good Morning America*, and *CBS Early Morning*. The American Association for Marriage and Family Therapy has selected him as a national conference plenary speaker and a Master's Series Therapist.

He is a professor of marriage and family therapy at Fuller Theological Seminary in Pasadena, California and is president and in practice at Amarillo Family Institute, Inc.

Sharon Hargrave is the executive director of the Boone Center for the Family at Pepperdine University in Malibu, California. She is a Licensed Marriage and Family Therapist in both California and Texas. She is also the founder of MarriageStrong at Fuller Theological Seminary in Pasadena, California.

Along with her husband, Sharon speaks nationally and internationally on issues pertaining to couples in ministry, marriage, intergenerational relationships, parenting and the restoration therapy model. She also works with couples in crisis with an intensive marital therapy model.

Sharon was in private practice working with couples and families for over eighteen years before she began her work with Fuller Seminary in 2008 and Pepperdine University in 2012. She specializes in working with marital and intergenerational issues. She and Terry have two married adult children.